W9-AHG-612

Quick!
The Cement Is Drying

101 Bits of Wisdom to Jump Start
Your Financial Services Career

Sabine Robinson, CLU

Copyright 2004 by Sabine Robinson

All rights reserved. No part of this book may be reproduced or transmitted in any form or by any means, electronic or mechanical, including photocopying, recording or by any information storage and retrieval system, without written permission from the author, except for the inclusion of brief quotations in a review.

Published by:
Ogunquit Press, Saint Louis, Missouri 63119 U.S.A.

ISBN:
0-9769457-0-3

Library of Congress Control Number:
2004107163

Printed in the United States of America
First Printing 2004

Cover Design: designlab,inc

Dedication

Dedicated to the memories of Martin Polhemus, CLU, and
T. Lynn Prewitt, CLU, two giants in the industry whose
impact will live on for generations.

Acknowledgements

There are so many people to whom I am grateful for so many things. This page recognizes those who directly or indirectly contributed to *Quick! The Cement Is Drying* becoming a reality.

First and foremost, thanks to my Mom and Dad who didn't think I was crazy for leaving my "real" job to start my own business and write a book. They have always believed in me.

Thanks to John Qualy, CLU, from whom I learned nearly everything I know about the financial services business. The result of his wisdom and teaching can be seen throughout these pages. In particular, the "Five Essential Beliefs" essay originated with John.

Thanks to Lee, Greg and Elizabeth Falk, intrepid entrepreneurs whose example encouraged me to venture out on my own. Special thanks to Lee, my wonderful friend and editor for her unconditional friendship and unerring eye for brevity and good grammar.

Thanks to Marcia Niekamp, CLU, ChFC, who, when I got stuck, revitalized this project with her enthusiasm for the material and introduced me to Lynne Klippel, my fabulous publisher.

Thanks to my fantastic study group: Sue Lewandowski, Tammy Palecek, Sheri Cox, Sheila Faust, Laura Kleinhans, Mary Ann Schachtner and Nita Hammett for their constant support---and for creating the opportunity in Maine to finally finish the book.

Thanks to Phil Bender who has always been a prime source of encouragement in my endeavors.

Thanks to all the agents I have coached and continue to coach for allowing me to learn from their experiences. Without them there wouldn't be a book.

Thanks to all the good people I have come to know over my years with the Northwestern Mutual Financial Network. It is a privilege to learn from the best.

Thanks to all my colleagues and friends for their unflagging encouragement and accountability and for never getting tired of asking, "How's the book coming?"

Thanks to my Tarsus Toastmasters friends, especially Bobbi Linkemer, Sharon Winstein and Fred Miller, all of whom have been relentless cheerleaders over the years.

And a special thanks to Jim Zara, CLU, ChFC, who planted the seed for this book when he said years ago at a training class lunch while discussing goals and vision, "If Bean really wanted to write a book, she'd write a book." Consider it done.

"I think the purpose of life is to be useful, to be responsible, to be honorable, to be compassionate. It is, after all, to matter, to count, to stand for something, to have made some difference that you lived at all."

LEO C. ROSTEN

Foreword

Since I first began working in the financial services industry in 1946, much has changed. The economy has gone through its cycles of highs and lows, dozens of new products have been introduced, and consumer values have shifted. However, the key factors influencing this business remain strong: It is still one of the most difficult careers you can choose, and it is still one of the most rewarding careers you can pursue --- both personally and financially.

This, too, remains true: I have always maintained that the right amount of the right kind of organized activity will inevitably yield results based on predictable relationships. This approach is just as reliable today as it was in 1969 when we first reported the early results of our research at the annual meeting of the Million Dollar Round Table.

Now comes this insightful book, *Quick! The Cement Is Drying*, to put forth "the rest of the story." Development Specialist Sabine Robinson has used her experience with some of the industry's most successful agents and agencies in the writing of this concise and inspirational book. She accurately sums up the emotional roller coaster that is a new agent's career, providing the guidance and encouragement vital to building a viable business.

Sabine's expertise and track record of coaching successful new agents shines through as she shares the legacy and learning that has guided leading producers for their entire careers.

Consider this a companion piece to *Building a Financial Services Clientele* and read them together to get the best possible start in a great career or to get a jump start for established careers. It promises you the emotional balance and support vital to a long, successful career in this, our chosen field.

O. ALFRED GRANUM, CLU

Introduction

Imagine, as a new agent, being able to instantly tap into the experience and wisdom of all the successful agents who have gone before you---from the sage encouragement of a retiring agent to a well-timed thump on the head from this year's highest producer. That's what this book is all about.

The concepts and advice contained within these pages span an entire career's worth of wisdom. Over time, you will hear these ideas from various sources, but imagine the power and confidence you gain from knowing them now. These are not sales ideas, but the underlying philosophies that have to be in place in order to build your sales skills as you progress. After all, the best sales idea in the world can't help you if you don't have the right mindset or attitude first.

Having worked with hundreds of new agents, I know that you are overwhelmed with everything you need to learn in the early months of your career. I also know that reading tends to get pushed to the bottom of the to-do list. With that in mind, I kept this material as easy to read and digest as possible. You can turn to any page in the book and in less than five minutes gain a valuable insight that will inspire you in your chosen career.

My goal is for you to realize that what you will feel and experience as you start out is normal. Nearly all others who have walked this path have felt and experienced the same things as they battled through the early part of their careers.

A special word to veteran agents: If you have reached a plateau in your journey, you may find it helpful to review these basic concepts that likely contributed to your initial success, but have since been relegated to dusty corners in your mind.

I hope these words will encourage you and lift you up during times of doubt and stress. I hope that as you progress in your career, you build a strong business and a solid character. Most of all, I hope that you will persevere through the obstacles to gain the incredible rewards that come from choosing a business in which you help yourself by helping others.

SABINE ROBINSON, CLU

#1 Get a Real Job

"To go against the dominant thinking of your friends, of most of the people you see every day, is perhaps the most difficult act of heroism you can perform."

THEODORE H. WHITE

When you initially announce your decision to come into this commission-only business, your family and friends will have mixed reactions. Some will encourage your new venture and willingly refer you to people they know, and some will look at you and say, "You've got to be kidding. Couldn't you get a real job?" You will likely experience more of the second reaction than the first.

This is your first test of conviction as you begin your career. Understand that most of the skepticism is out of caring and concern for your welfare. Another part of the puzzlement is often because many others would never dream of taking the risk you are about to take and can't understand why anyone would. People who aren't in the business don't know much about it except that more people fail than succeed. Then there are those who are envious of your courage and will subtly attempt to undermine your decision by constantly planting seeds of doubt.

It's natural to believe that everyone in your circle will wish you well in your new career and, in turn, will readily meet with you. Be prepared: Not all of them will. The best way to handle the situation is to let your success speak for itself. Proving the skeptics wrong can be a compelling motivation to work hard and build a solid business quickly.

Sometimes it's more difficult to work with people you know and perhaps grew up with. They may have a difficult time sharing confidential information or seeing you in this different role. Often the sooner you get out of this "natural" market, the better.

By choosing this career, you are breaking away from the crowd. You are forging a new, more difficult, yet rewarding life. Instead of worrying about what the skeptics are saying, stay focused on your mission. Soon you will be able to face them and say, "What do you think now?"

#2 CEO, Receptionist and Janitor

"Success on any major scale requires you to take responsibility. In the final analysis, the one quality all successful people have is the ability to take on responsibility."

MICHAEL KORDA

Being in business for themselves is a fantasy that most people entertain periodically. You have taken the leap and are actually doing it. Now reality sets in...including the fact that not only are you the CEO, CFO and president, but you are also the secretary, receptionist and janitor. At least in the beginning. True, you have the freedom and flexibility and no boss, but (and this is a big but) you also have all the responsibility...100 percent of it.

When things don't go as you want, you have only one place to look and that is at your own reflection. It sounds glamorous to be in business for yourself, but in reality it is a lot of hard work, discipline and sweat. You don't get to enjoy the rewards on a large scale until you have been at it for quite a while. It's a double-edged sword – you eventually get all the good stuff, but you also have to deal with all the junk along the way. An unhappy client calls in – guess who fields the call? Trash can overflowing – guess who gets to empty it? Quarterly taxes need to be paid – guess who writes the check?

When you are making this decision, be sure you look at both sides. Those who are in business for themselves love it, but understand it isn't all a bed of roses. If you are willing to play all roles, even the less desirable ones, in the early stages then you have a chance at success. If you only want the up side, you'll be out of business in the blink of an eye.

#3 Be Prepared

"When you are afraid, keep your mind on what you have to do. And if you have been thoroughly prepared, you will not be afraid."

DALE CARNEGIE

The recruiting and selection process for candidates coming into the business is a lengthy one. This is good news for you – if you use this time to your advantage. It means that both you and your potential company have ample opportunity to evaluate each other and see if it's a good fit. This time also allows you to put away some money to get started. This is one of the few businesses that don't require a large startup investment (like a buying a franchise would), but it is enormously helpful to have at least three months of living expenses put aside. This gives you the peace of mind in the early days to stay focused on your activity.

Three months of living expenses is a good measure: It's enough to get started, but not enough to cause complacency. Having some financial incentive (such as paying bills) is healthy to your business growth. It can fuel your desire to earn income quickly. Very few people come into the business not needing to make money right away. In fact, those who don't have an economic incentive often take longer to get going. They don't have the need for income driving them forward through the obstacles, and they tend to procrastinate and become paralyzed by fear.

However, if you are so strapped that you can't put away a short-term financial cushion, then you might re-evaluate your decision to come into the business until your situation improves. You will probably make a few sales right away to friends and family members, but it will take a few weeks to generate the activity that will yield results outside your natural market.

This isn't meant to deter you from this career choice, but rather to make sure you are realistic about the financial end of things.

#4 Read the Fine Print

"The will to succeed is important, but what's even more important is the will to prepare."

BOBBY KNIGHT

As you become affiliated with a company, you will be required to sign a contract. Make it your personal responsibility to read it and understand how it works. Part of being a business owner means understanding how you get paid, what your responsibilities are and what the company's responsibilities are. If there are bonuses for hitting certain production requirements or other incentives at different levels of production, you certainly want to know about them.

You probably have a copy of your contract which is now stuffed in a drawer somewhere or under the bed gathering dust. Pull it out now and read it, or re-read it. What are the expectations regarding performance, under what circumstances can you be terminated, what happens to your clients if you quit, and what can you do and not do within the confines of your contract?

It's also important for you to understand how to read your commission statement each pay period. This document tracks your year-to-date income, expenses charged, bonuses received and benefits. It also usually includes a client-by-client list of commissions paid.

It may not be the most exciting read, but you should have a thorough understanding of the contract you signed so that down the road there are no misunderstandings on your part or your company's part.

#5 Let Go of the Score

"Achievers give more than they get. They operate without a scorecard. Their enthusiasm and effort propel them forward and over time they become the leaders to look up to."

KIM SMITHSON

There are two kinds of giving people in the world: Those who give abundantly without a second thought and those who mentally keep track of every good deed done or gift given, expecting a one-to-one return for their effort. It seems like any kind of giving should be considered a good thing, and that's generally true. But have you ever been the recipient of a good deed or gift and felt that the giver wanted continuous recognition or was expecting something in return later? That you would prefer to give back whatever you received because the aftermath wasn't worth it?

People with a true abundance mentality don't keep score. They know intuitively that what they give will come back to them at some future time. With regard to clients, you will always give more than you receive. When you are selling an intangible product with built-in delayed gratification, the recognition you deserve won't come for a long time, if at all. Most clients won't thank you at the moment of sale for your work. They see another bill to pay, financial or lifestyle sacrifices to be made. Until someone dies, becomes disabled or needs to use your products in some way, they won't really appreciate the work you have done.

That's why you can't go through life keeping score. If you expect each prospect to become a client and each client to be incredibly grateful after every sale, you'll constantly be disappointed. Give everything you have in each meeting, believing that you've left each person better than before. Do your best for everyone and don't worry about the outcome; the rewards will multiply when you least expect it.

#6 The Great Equalizer

"Perhaps the most valuable result of all education is the ability to make yourself do the thing you have to do when it ought to be done, whether you like it or not."

THOMAS H. HUXLEY

People come into the financial services business from a variety of other careers, some sales-related, some not. It is helpful but not necessary to have prior sales experience. Regardless of which camp you fall into, this business is a totally different experience because of the intangible nature of its products. Some of your previous experience will translate, and some will not. Some former habits will help you, others will need to be forgotten.

The financial services business is a great equalizer. You must accept this fact early: The activity required to be successful applies to you regardless of your age or previous business experience. The law of large numbers to small numbers applies to the marketplace whether you are working with affluent or middle-income prospects. Income level does not equal propensity to buy.

If you have 20 years of business experience, that's great. It's an advantage because you may be able to get going faster than most, but you must still have the activity. If you just graduated from college and this is your first career, you must have the activity. It will always be a business of large numbers to small numbers, and your willingness to accept this fact will make your life much easier.

Some people with prior sales experience come into this business thinking the high activity rule doesn't apply to them. They spend the first year or so trying to reinvent the wheel, only to realize the wheel already invented works pretty well. But in the meantime they've wasted valuable time and cemented bad habits. Some people never get it, and leave the business scratching their head and wondering what went wrong. Believe in high activity early on, and you will succeed much more quickly.

#7 It's a Marathon, Not a Sprint

"The race goes not always to the swift...but to those who keep on running."

AUTHOR UNKNOWN

Nothing worth accomplishing comes easily. This business has more in common with a marathon than a sprint. There will be some sprints along the way, but the journey itself is a marathon – make no mistake about it. The steps required for both endeavors are similar.

It starts with a decision to enter the race. Then the training process begins. For a first-time marathoner, this means being able to run at least three miles. For a first-time agent it means learning the required language, the products and obtaining at least 100 names of people to call on. As the training progresses, marathoners will gradually increase their mileage. When they reach about 15 miles, it becomes increasingly difficult, both to physically run and to mentally stay in the game. The marathoners are battling fatigue, boredom and distractions in an effort to stay on track.

When first-time agents begin calling on people they've never met and experiencing rejection, they struggle in similar ways. They battle fear, call-reluctance and distractions in an effort to stay on track. It would be easy for both the marathoner and the new agent to give up at the first signs of struggle. Those with the mental discipline to persevere realize it is in the struggle that the victory is made.

When a marathoner crosses the finish line, the feeling of exhilaration outweighs the struggle of the journey. When an agent qualifies for the Million Dollar Round Table for the first time, the same feeling occurs. The formation of character is in the quest for victory, not in the victory itself.

#8 Put on Your Rose-Colored Glasses

"I will say this about being an optimist – even when things don't turn out well, you are certain they will get better."

FRANK HUGHES

The cliché "your attitude determines your altitude" is 100 percent correct. Most clichés have a fair amount of truth in them – that's why they became clichés in the first place. How you choose to look at the world every day will determine the majority of your success or failure. Your attitude is one of the only things over which you have complete control. Only you can decide what thoughts you will think. Your thoughts may be triggered by some external stimulus, but then you can choose to accept or reject whatever comes into your mind.

Your attitude is also the lens through which you see the rest of the world, and in turn it determines how the rest of the world sees you. If you are crabby, surly, rude and cynical, chances are you will see others as being the same. You will seek data to confirm your suspicions, which will color the way you interpret your experiences. You see how this can become a vicious cycle.

Why not make it a positive cycle? If you expect the best out of others, chances are they will live up to your expectations. You won't find many top sales people with negative attitudes. In fact, you will find them to be annoyingly positive most of the time. Plenty of negative things happen to these positive people, they just choose to see them from the "glass is half full" perspective. It's a much more pleasant way to go through your career and your life.

#9 Dress for Success

"Always bear in mind that your resolution to succeed is more important than any other thing."
ABRAHAM LINCOLN

People will seldom write big checks for your products if they don't trust you. The initial step toward building that trust is the first impression you make: your appearance. The reality of "don't judge a book by its cover" is that people do it all the time. Literally, in fact. Those who sell books to bookstores only bring the outer covers because they know that's what draws attention on the shelf.

If you are the smartest person in the financial services world, but don't look sharp when you show up, you have already lost ground. Golf shirts and khakis might be acceptable when you are meeting with a long-time client who prefers casual dress. However, when you first meet a prospect, it is wise to make a professional appearance. For men this means a suit and tie, for women it means a business suit. When it comes to being taken seriously in the business world, too much skin or a dress shirt without a t-shirt is always inappropriate.

Remember: You have chosen a fairly conservative business - you should dress accordingly. Comb your hair, shine your shoes, keep your nails clean and short, and leave the excess jewelry at home. When you attain a Bill Gates or Steven Spielberg level of success and have a reputation as THE person someone wants to see, then you can go to appointments in jeans and a t-shirt if you wish. Until then, dress for success. You will feel more confident when you know you are dressed appropriately.

#10 Likeability – It Matters

"If people respect you but don't like you, they won't stay with you. If they like you but don't respect you, they will stay with you but they won't follow you. To be an effective leader, you must earn both from your people."

JOHN MAXWELL

Your ability to get along with others will make the path to success much smoother. This doesn't mean telling people what they want to hear, spewing forth insincere flattery or constantly currying favor with others. It simply means developing the ability to listen sincerely, apply a degree of compassion and diplomacy to your words and extend common courtesies on a daily basis.

Most other things being equal, people will tend to buy from people they like. How would people answer the following questions about you? "Would I have this person in my home?" "Would I be comfortable introducing this person to my friends and family?" "Would I buy anything from this person?" These questions are often asked internally in the recruiting process to get a gut feeling about how a person will come across to others. You will spend a fair amount of time in other peoples' homes and offices, and how comfortable they are with you will partially determine their willingness to buy and refer others.

There are numerous ways to learn more about the art of getting along with others. Investing in a Dale Carnegie course, joining Toastmasters (a public speaking group) or simply reading a book or two can give you a head start. Asking for feedback from people who know and have worked with you can also give you valuable information about how you are perceived.

Don't underestimate the "likeability" factor in the sales process. If you are a likeable person, continue to develop your skills. If you need help in this area, get started right away. It's one of the key areas you can develop in your career.

#11 Believe It – Then You'll See It

"When you absolutely have to land that plane, there will be a runway – even if you can't see it sometimes."

JOHN HAMM

There is a scene in the movie "Indiana Jones and the Last Crusade" where the title character stands on the edge of a precipice and must cross over it in order to save his father's life. Just one problem: There's no bridge. However, Indiana Jones knows he has to believe that the bridge will appear when he needs it so he takes a deep breath and steps out. And guess what? The bridge appears under his feet with the first step.

This business is a lot like that. You must have that element of belief that the marketplace will respond if you are continuously engaged in the right activities – that if you risk taking that step, the bridge will appear. Sometimes people will go through the motions of a particular activity with no belief that it will yield results. They are determined to disprove ideas and usually end up fulfilling their own prophecies.

Those who believe that good results will follow their efforts also wind up fulfilling their own prophecies. It's been suggested that the adage "I'll believe it when I see it" be changed to "I'll see it when I believe it." There comes a moment of truth when you have to move forward without knowing exactly what the outcome will be, without perfect circumstances, with nothing but the wholehearted belief that you are on the right course and that the desired result will appear at the right moment.

When you summon the courage to take that step, rest assured the bridge will appear.

#12 The Path Is There – Follow It

"Others have done it before me. I can too."

CORPORAL JOHN FAUNCE

There are times when it is necessary to be original and times when it is best to follow in the footsteps of those who have preceded you. It is important to know the difference.

On the life insurance side of the financial services business, the system designed by O. Alfred Granum, CLU, for client building has yet to be improved upon. On the investment side of the business, the writings of Nick Murray provide tremendous guidance. Both of these bodies of knowledge are based on years of research, observation and experience.

You can accelerate your learning curve by putting your energy into following these systems rather than trying to create your own. The Granum system in particular requires hard work and lots of it. The temptation to think you can find a better, easier system will inevitably pass through your mind – ignore it and get back to work.

Save your creativity and originality for finding solutions to your clients' problems. Following a proven system affords you more freedom, not less. Having structure gives you one less thing to worry about. Think of it as a safety net. You don't have to spend your time wondering what to do next – you can focus instead on the needs of your clients and prospects.

Great ideas withstand the test of time and both Granum and Murray have proven theirs work. You will succeed much faster if you don't resist these systems, but embrace them and then relish the results.

#13 Risky Business – Part 1

"Progress always involves risk. You can't steal second and keep your foot on first."

FREDERICK WILCOX

The only real path to freedom involves risk. All who have accomplished great things have taken great risks, personally, professionally, emotionally and financially. You have put yourself on that path by choosing this business. Your capacity for risk will determine your future success.

Risk does not mean making rash decisions or taking careless actions without regard for danger. Risk is the ability to assess a situation and move toward a goal, comfortable with the fact that there are elements you can't control. It means making bold moves in pursuit of your purpose without perfect circumstances or a 100 percent guaranteed outcome. You must be more committed to progress than perfection.

You know risk is in the air when you get that same feeling in your stomach as you get on the downhill part of the roller coaster ride. Scary? Yes, but exhilarating in the end – so much so that you usually want to do it over and over again once you've conquered it the first time.

Embrace risk; don't hide from it or attempt to outsmart it. Imagine it is the sentry guarding the door to your goal. The only way in is through that door, not over it, under it or around it.

#14 Risky Business – Part 2

"While one person hesitates because he feels inferior, the other is busy making mistakes and becoming superior."

HENRY C. LINK

People in this business tend to spend lots of time trying to eliminate or decrease the risks, particularly the risk of rejection. It can be an awful feeling to be told "no" when you have put yourself on the line. However, no one ever died from being told "no" in a business setting. When you have a large number of prospects to call on, you lessen the pain of each "no."

Imagine you are in your office. In the reception area are hundreds of people waiting, with more arriving all the time. You ask them one by one if they would be interested in your services. When someone says "no" you thank him or her politely and call out "next," secure in the knowledge that there will always be more. Mentally shake your head sadly when someone tells you "no," say to yourself, "their loss," then move on. After all, the waiting room is full.

Nancy, a successful agent, imagines an abundance of prospects as she sits in traffic or at a ballgame and notices the thousands of people around her. It doesn't mean she's never scared or doesn't have that roller coaster feeling in the pit of her stomach. It just means she constantly tells herself that there are plenty of people out there and she has to risk a few "no's" to get to the lucky ones who will say "yes" and get to work with her.

This abundance mentality goes a long way towards making risk an ally and not an enemy.

#15 It's Possible to Have Good Debt

"The sea is dangerous and its storms terrible, but these obstacles have never been sufficient reason to remain ashore."

FERDINAND MAGELLAN

Choosing to be self-employed means you have to have the stomach for risk. A significant part of that risk is financial. All business owners who are growing have business debt. The crucial factor is whether it's debt incurred for business growth or debt incurred because of poor financial management or because of living beyond your means. You must become comfortable with the idea that you may have to borrow money to get started or to grow to the next level. If you are a person who has never had debt before, this will require some soul-searching. Letting go of the idea that you can operate a growing business debt-free is crucial.

Incurring debt and paying it off is a normal business cycle. Understanding and believing that will help you spend your mental energy on growing your business instead of getting stuck in panic mode because you now have some debt.

Remember, you are not on a fixed income. Through increased activity you can out-produce your expenses and debts. One top-producing agent tells the story of when he started in the business as a newlywed; his wife became pregnant with their first child and wanted to stay home full time. He panicked at first because of the lost income but then he figured out he could replace her income by selling one more policy per month. Remembering this abundance perspective is critical to your success.

#16 What "Fake It 'Til You Make It" Really Means

"You are more likely to act yourself into feeling than feel yourself into action."

JEROME BRUNER

You may often hear the phrase "fake it 'til you make it" from veterans in the business. This doesn't mean buying what you can't afford or living a lifestyle you haven't yet earned. It really applies to overcoming fear through action. "Faking" refers to conjuring a feeling you don't yet have so you can take the action that's causing the fear. For example, when you feel anxiety as you are about to make your phone calls, you can "fake" how excited you are to be engaging in this particular activity. Once you get started and make your first appointment, the feeling you "faked" is no longer a false feeling – it's the real thing.

Action always precedes feeling. If you wait until you feel like doing something you don't want to do, you'll never get it done. On the flip side, if you just start doing the dreaded task, the feeling of accomplishment will naturally surface. When it's over, you will be elated. Action creates the feeling.

Many purposely misinterpret the phrase "Fake it 'til you make it." It's easier than thinking about what it really means. On the surface, it can be seen to mean go buy yourself a Rolex or an expensive car so people will have the perception you are already wealthy and successful. However, driving yourself into debt to create a false image just creates more stress. Now you are burdened not only with debts you can't pay, but also with the nagging feeling of "What if they find out?"

Next time someone says to you "Fake it 'til you make it," ask them to explain what they mean and see which interpretation they give. This will help you to filter their comments appropriately.

#17 Why Not?

"I swing big, with everything I've got. I hit big or I miss big. I like to live as big as I can."

BABE RUTH

If you are going to be in a business of unlimited income and opportunity, you need to develop the habit of thinking *BIG*. This may not be natural at first, especially if you come from a fixed-income position where it didn't matter how big you thought, your paycheck would still be the same. Now you have the chance to directly affect your income and your life, and it starts with your thinking.

Thinking big is about more than just large amounts of money. It is about all the things you want to do in your life. A great exercise in thinking big is to make a list of 100 things you want to do before you die. They can be crazy, outrageous, fun, challenging, simple or seemingly impossible. Just write down everything that comes to mind, no matter how off-the-wall it seems. You can do this with your spouse, your family or by yourself. Then ask yourself, "Why not?"

"Why not?" is a great question to ponder whenever you think something is unrealistic. Most big ideas can be broken down into a series of small steps, which suddenly make the seemingly impossible more realistic. For example, most people who have completed a marathon thought at one time that it was a crazy idea, but by following a systematic program were able to finish.

Next time you have a thought that causes you to shake your head while thinking, "Nah," reverse the trend and ask yourself instead, "Why not?"

#18 Yoda and the Financial Services Business

Luke Skywalker: "Alright. I'll give it a try."
Yoda: "No! Try not. Do. Or do not. There is no "try.""

GEORGE LUCAS'S FILM
"Star Wars: The Empire Strikes Back"

The old adage "Sticks and stones may break my bones but words will never hurt me" is a myth. Words have immense power. They can hurt, heal, encourage, inspire, move people to action and change lives. They have a definite impact on your psyche. That's why it is critical to monitor the words you use when making commitments. There are also words it's better to do without – permanently.

Words that dilute your commitments include try, might, would, should and could among others. "Try" is the worst offender and the first word to eliminate from your daily vocabulary. It weakens any sentence in which it appears. Here's an exercise to prove it. Lay a pen on your desk. Now "try" to pick it up. The pen will either remain on your desk or it will be in your hand. There is no in-between. It doesn't hover magically between your desk and hand in an attempt to be either place.

Imagine getting to the altar with your intended and in the ceremony saying, "I'll *try* to commit for the rest of my life." Or having the person who recruited you say, "We'll *try* to make sure you have all the resources you need to succeed." There is no commitment in the word "try." It simply leaves room for excuses and backpedaling.

Would, could and should also weaken language. They imply "if" or "but." "I would do that if...I could do that if...I should do that but..." Conditional language creates doubt. When you replace these words with "I will," not only do you make a stronger commitment, you literally feel differently. You inspire confidence in yourself and others and are more motivated to then do the thing you committed to. It is a simple but powerful tool to create integrity.

#19 If You Want to Move Up, Move Out

"Have a dream so big that you cannot achieve it until you grow into the person who can!"

ANONYMOUS

This is written for a specific group of people who are living at home with their parents in an effort to save money. If you fall into this category, you are facing a cruel irony. This method of saving money may also prevent you from making money as quickly as you would like. Why? It's difficult to take someone seriously as a businessperson when they are living at home with mom and dad. Although your prospects may not know it, you know it and it can put a dent in your confidence.

Being on your own in the adult world where you have expenses and responsibilities helps you relate better to your prospects and clients. It also gives you the incentive to produce business or you risk not being able to pay your bills. You have to be willing to trade comfort for risk. Maybe you can't buy your own house just yet, but you can certainly rent a decent apartment and establish good credit. You are teaching your prospects and clients by your own example.

"But I can't afford to move out yet," you cry in despair. Stop that thinking and focus on possible solutions. Then make a plan and start chipping away at it. Maybe this is the time to establish a line of credit or take out a short-term loan. Maybe your parents will loan you enough to get through the first month. Whatever your particular solution is, you can't afford to wait. If this risk is uncomfortable for you, good – it's mild compared to what's coming.

The sooner you are willing to face the world standing on your own two feet, the sooner you will make a quantum leap forward in your quest for success. The independence you gain will fuel your confidence and hasten your journey to prosperity.

#20 Every Day Is a Do-Over

"Remember, you will not always win. Some days, the most resourceful individual will taste defeat. But there is, in this case, always tomorrow – after you have done your best to achieve success today."

DR. MAXWELL MALTZ

Beginning each day with a clean slate is a state of mind. You can't change what you did or didn't do the day before or the previous week. All you can do is begin again. If something isn't working the way you want it to, wipe the slate clean and start over.

Each day that you get up and get to work is an opportunity to start fresh. If you truly believe this, it will make the bad days easier to bear and the good days that much better.

If you are in a slump, pretend that the next day is your very first day out of training all over again. Begin as if you were brand new to the business. But now you have the benefit of some missteps from which to learn. You can have the best of both worlds – you can live the "If I only knew then what I know now" wish because now you do know it.

It's a trick of the mind, but a powerful one if you put it to use. You are able to learn from your mistakes and clear the way to attaining your goals. It's a great way to halt a downward spiral. Otherwise, you find yourself indulging in regret or wishful thinking on a daily basis. You get stuck in the thought that "if I'd only done this or that" things would be better. In reality, things will be better if you hit the mental "reset" button and start again.

Don't confuse hitting the mental "reset" button with the "rewind" button. Rewinding implies going backward and repeating, whereas resetting means starting fresh from where you are right now. Developing this mental habit can get you moving forward again in the right direction.

#21 Forward Progress Every Day

"Growth is not a steady, upward progression. It is instead a switchback trail; three steps forward, two back, one around the bushes, and a few simply standing, before another forward leap."

DOROTHY CORKVILLE BRIGGS

In a perfect world, your business would travel a smooth, upward trajectory for many years without ever dropping off or hitting a plateau. However, in the real world, it's not that simple. Your business will develop in fits and starts, with a quantum leap thrown in every now and then. The overall result is forward progress, but not without a few backward steps.

Don't be discouraged by setbacks. It's a natural part of growing a business. You can minimize the impact of the downward cycles through constant activity. As chaos swirls around you, you can cut through the fog of uncertainty with the sharp knife of activity. It's the only constant that you can control and the one sure way to reverse a downward trend.

When you are up, you need consistent activity and when you are down, you need consistent activity even more. There's just no escaping that fact. After a good week or a good month, you will be tempted to let up just a little – don't do it. It only takes a couple of weeks for a slow down in activity to catch up with you and when it does, it's painful. You will be taken by surprise and then have to work twice as hard to get things going again.

Save yourself the aggravation and keep your activity constant through good times and bad. Remember, you are in this for the long haul. It's about steady progress, not perfection.

#22 Five Essential Beliefs

*"You are embarking on the greatest adventure of your life –
to improve your self-image, to create more meaning in your
life and in the lives of others. This is your responsibility.
Accept it, now!"*

DR. MAXWELL MALTZ

The following five beliefs will give you a structure on which to build your business philosophy. They are essential ingredients in your success. When you falter, consult these five tenets to see in which area you need to improve.

1. Belief in your company. Presumably, most of you have this one down or you wouldn't be where you are in the first place. It is virtually impossible to sell something when you don't believe in the company.

2. Belief in your products. The surest way to demonstrate this belief is to own a substantial amount of what you are selling. You can say you believe in your products, but until you become your own best client, your words will ring hollow.

3. Belief in your value as an agent. This is the one where new agents in particular struggle. It is difficult to see your value until someone becomes disabled or dies and you are there to deliver the proceeds. You have to accept this delayed gratification. This requires some faith on your part – belief without tangible evidence.

4. Belief in a system of activity. Whether it is the Granum system or another system that your company espouses, you must believe and adopt it. If your predecessors used it successfully, don't waste your time and energy trying to better it.

5. Belief in goal attainment - not just goal setting but putting in the effort to achieve those goals. You must believe that you can and will attain your goals.

If you will adopt these five beliefs and use them as general checkpoints you will have a much better chance of staying the course.

#23 This Stuff Won't Sell Itself

"Treat people as if they were what they ought to be and you help them to become what they are capable of being."
JOHANN WOLFGANG VON GOETHE

Financial products are not bought, they are sold, particularly insurance products. People will not seek you out because they don't realize they need your products until it is too late. You are overcoming resistance at every step in the sales cycle – from getting the initial prospect, making the appointment, completing the factfinder to finally closing the sale. Do not kid yourself that these products will sell themselves. They won't. It is a sales business, and you will need to develop sales skills.

Insurance products are intangible products; you are selling what it does, not what it is. To the eye, insurance is just a piece of paper with a promise on it. Your client can't touch, smell, feel, taste or spend that in any tangible way – until you bring cash to the table because they lived too long, died too soon, chose to retire early or became disabled. Then it changes people's lives.

There is a place in the world for all kinds of financial products, but insurance products are the backbone of a solid financial plan. If you don't believe this, then you will have a tough time in the business. Every time the market crashes, plain-vanilla whole life insurance is the only thing some people have left. Doing the right thing means first protecting what people have built, then helping taking more risk with their money in investments.

#24 It's All in Your Head

"I cannot always control what goes on outside. But I can always control what goes on inside."

WAYNE DYER

In psychology there is a concept known as "locus of control." People tend toward an internal locus of control or an external locus of control. The difference between the two is where you believe the responsibility for what happens in your life lies.

In the book, *The Non-Runner's Marathon Trainer*, there is a succinct explanation of this concept. "...it doesn't matter whether the events in your life are REALLY in your control or not; it only matters whether you THINK they are."

In other words, if you think you have some measure of control, you will try to exercise it regularly and thus influence events. If you don't believe you have any control, you will sit back and do nothing, thereby allowing whatever happens to happen without any input from you. The ability to create your own internal reality can have a profound influence on how you proceed day to day.

Any long-term endeavor requiring discipline must begin with an internal locus of control. If the word "control" bothers you, then substitute the word "influence." While you can't "control" anything, you can "influence" everything.

#25 That Messy First Year

"Every worthwhile accomplishment, big or little, has its stages of drudgery and triumph; a beginning, a struggle and a victory."

AUTHOR UNKNOWN

The first year isn't about grace, beauty or skill. It is about survival, guts and the will to persevere in the face of every obstacle. The first year is the hardest, especially when you have chosen a field where the pay is strictly commission. You must build everything from scratch. If you do a good job in year one, in subsequent years you will have a solid client base upon which to continue building.

The first year is about laying the foundation for future years. If you don't do what is required in year one, subsequent years will be just as difficult, if not more so. The beginning is exciting, and most people are filled with enthusiasm until they get out of training and into the field. It is in these stages of struggle that many are tempted to give up...and do.

There is a tremendous learning curve in the first year. Everything feels awkward and most new agents are unsure of themselves because they have never done anything like this before. Those who are willing to risk making mistakes and learning from them will outshine everyone else in the end. If you can take each day as it comes and stick it out through that first year, you will have survived one of the most vulnerable periods in your career.

#26 By Design or By Default

"The people who get on in this world are the people who get up and look for the circumstances they want, and if they can't find them, make them."

GEORGE BERNARD SHAW

Everything is a choice. One of the first things you have to understand is the concept of self-determination. Some people believe they can impact their destiny; others believe their destiny depends on external circumstances. The first group lives by design, the second by default.

Those who believe they can influence their destiny decide how they want life to unfold and go to work to make it happen. Those who only react to situations wait to see what happens and then tailor their excuses to fit the particular circumstances.

Andrew and Karen are new agents; each sets a goal to write 100 policies in the upcoming year. Karen commits to the goal and begins to visualize the result. She lists her open cases and figures out how many people she will have to see, how many referred leads she will need and how many policies she will have to write each month. She thinks about what she will have to change in her process since this is new to her. Each day she asks herself "What can I do today to move closer to my goal?"

Andrew says he wants to write 100 policies but immediately begins to list the obstacles. He has so many meetings to attend, his closing ratio isn't the best, he doesn't have enough people to call, he is in two weddings, etc. He says he will do his best to write 100 policies, but it will depend on how things work out.

At the end of the year, it is likely that Karen will have accomplished her goal due to her daily focus, her planning and her attitude. Andrew will probably fall short and have an air-tight list of excuses. The excuses will sound legitimate and Andrew will be satisfied that he did his best, even though he didn't reach his goal. Karen will most likely go on to build a successful business. Andrew will probably leave the business or be consistently mediocre.

Karen designed her success. Andrew defaulted to easy excuses.

#27 Working Hard or Hardly Working

"Nothing worthwhile comes easily. Half effort does not produce half results. It produces no results. Work, continuous work and hard work, is the only way to accomplish results that last."

HAMILTON HOLT

The habit of working hard is a character trait. You either have it or you don't. If you have developed the habit of putting forth minimum effort in your life endeavors, you won't suddenly become a hard worker. Conversely, if you have disciplined yourself to work hard at the things you want to accomplish, you will naturally bring that trait to this career. Hard work is essential. You will not succeed in the financial services business without it. It is the best way to battle the overwhelming number of times you will hear "no."

The question "What is hard work?" has many answers. Hard work is a combination of several factors. The first is disciplining yourself to consistently do what is required when it is required. The second is doing more than is required when the situation demands it. And the third is following through and finishing what you start without making excuses.

Hard work is not about simply putting in long hours, although that is often required. It is easy to delude yourself into thinking you are "working hard" simply because you spent 12 hours at the office or on the road. The key is spending those hours on tasks that will yield results, thus moving your business forward.

Working hard precedes working smart. Its human nature to want to do things more efficiently, but there is no short-cut to efficiency. Efficiency is the result of constant repetition and adjustments.

#28 The Freedom Account

"The golden opportunity you are seeking is in yourself. It is not in your environment, it is not in luck or chance or the help of others; it is in yourself alone."

ORISON SWETT MARDEN

It is a fact: You can't have the freedom self-employment offers without the discipline it requires. It's early career death to think otherwise. Freedom and flexibility are often cited as the main reasons people want to come into this business. The notion of not having a traditional boss or traditional hours is more important to most people than the money. Freedom is the dangling carrot enticing you to leap into a commission-only business where your success or failure depends entirely on you.

Getting paid exactly what you are worth can be a positive or a negative. Visualize your freedom as a bank account where you make a deposit every time you forgo an opportunity during the work week to play golf, go shopping, go fishing, or take an afternoon off in the first three to five years. The discipline required to give up those temptations will cause your freedom deposits to grow and compound for future use. Meanwhile, your business is also compounding from your decision to work when you could have been playing.

Bob, a veteran agent, happens to love deep-sea fishing. Because he worked hard early and built a solid foundation, he is now able to take six months off every year to go deep-sea fishing around the world. His freedom account is paying huge dividends today from deposits he made in the early years.

#29 Rookie Jitters

"Believe in yourself! Have faith in your abilities! Without a humble, but reasonable confidence in your own powers, you cannot be successful or happy."
NORMAN VINCENT PEALE

When you've never done something before, there is always an element of doubt about whether you can really do it. Once you accomplish something for the first time however, that element disappears and you are forever changed. Every accomplishment shifts something inside of you and sets the bar a little higher. Your mind now knows that you can do that particular thing and won't let you forget it.

The hardest part of any new accomplishment is doing it for the first time. Then each subsequent time you have the confidence of the preceding victory to provide the forward momentum. By the time you've done something for the 8th or 10th or 50th time, that's a lot of confidence. You will still have the adrenaline rush of going into the task, but you will also have the confidence of knowing you have done it many times before with a successful outcome. It then becomes somewhat predictable.

In this way you build a base of positive results, and results breed confidence. It might be making a new phone call, giving a speech before a group or telling someone how you feel about something that makes you uncomfortable. Every time you do it, it becomes more familiar to you and less frightening. You can build on small successes and eventually even the scariest tasks will have less power over you.

#30 Resist Temptation

"Character cannot be developed in ease and quiet. Only through experience of trial and suffering can the soul be strengthened, ambition inspired and success achieved."
HELEN KELLER

In any difficult endeavor there will be the temptation to take short cuts. The temptation increases in proportion to the difficulty of the endeavor. Therefore, the temptation to take short cuts in this business is overwhelming. Resist, resist, resist, all the while remembering that the harder the endeavor, the sweeter the reward.

The reason you can make a lot of money in this business is because it is so difficult. You must be willing to face the fear and rejection that others choose not to. If it were easy, people would be lined up to sign contracts, and no one would be making any money. Look around: Usually the more difficult something is, the more income potential there is associated with it.

Tempted to mail your policies rather than deliver them in person because you think it's a waste of time? Remember, frequency of contact with your clients makes them less likely to replace what they bought or replace you as their agent. Tempted to initial or sign for someone so you can avoid an extra trip to get a missed signature? It's illegal and could cost you your contract and your career. Tempted to sell a product to someone with no need in order to qualify for an award or contest? Remember, these kinds of sales result in lapsed policies.

There's no shortcut in this marathon of a business – you have to start at the beginning and stay the course until you cross the finish line. Remember this when you are tempted to do anything other than what your company trained you to do. When you succeed, it is made much sweeter by the degree of difficulty. You will seldom feel that good about doing something anyone could have done.

#31 Quick! The Cement Is Drying

"What we do today, right now, will have an accumulated effect on all our tomorrows."

ALEXANDRA STODDARD

The first year of your career is by far the hardest, and the first six months of that year are critical to forming good habits. Seldom do agents fall away from good habits established early, and conversely, few overcome bad habits established during the early months. Sean, a highly successful agent, once said "You can be a third-year agent in your first year, or you can be a first-year agent in your third year." Certainly some agents with less-than-stellar habits manage to survive through sheer determination, but during the course of their careers, they are constantly reliving that difficult first year.

Imagine pouring wet cement. In its initial state, the cement is easy to form and re-form. As it dries, with every minute that goes by, it becomes more difficult to change the form. By the time it's completely dry, it takes a jackhammer to break it apart. Putting it into a different form at this point is possible but certainly difficult, and the result looks patched together and does not hold as well over time.

Your habits are the same way. Early on, when everything is new, habits are easier to form and re-form. The longer a habit goes (good or bad), the harder it is to break. If you talk to a successful agent, chances are they haven't deviated too much from the habits they formed in their first six months. Likewise, if you interview someone who is struggling in their second or third year, they are probably paying the price for poor habits established early. Pay close attention to those first six months and establish the right habits for long-term success before the cement dries.

#32 More No's Equals More Yes's

"Success is not final, failure is not fatal; it is the courage to continue that counts."

SIR WINSTON CHURCHILL

At the risk of repetition, the first six months are a critical window of time. This business needs to be front-end loaded with activity to yield the best results over time. If you can sell 40 policies in the first six months of your contract, you significantly enhance your chances for long-term success and retention. Less than 10 percent of new agents accomplish this goal because of the sheer amount of work involved. This is always a business of large numbers to small numbers, so to get to 40 policies sold requires a large amount of kept appointments and factfinding interviews.

While 40 policies in six months significantly enhances your chance for success, 100 policies in your first 12 months virtually guarantees it. If this sounds like a lot of work, it is. Nothing worthwhile comes without significant effort and struggle. 100 lives in 12 months equals 8.3 lives per month or two lives per week. Consistent high activity is the best way to get to the two people per week who will say "yes." Because if you will recall, not everyone will buy from you.

Those who lead in number of policies sold usually also lead in number of times they are told "no." But they persist because they know that once they start getting a large number of "no's," they will get some "yes's." They are willing to wade through the rejection to get what's on the other side. Hearing "no" enough times to get 40 prospects to say "yes" in six months or 100 prospects to say "yes" in your first year will give you confidence. Repeating this feat year after year and building on it will bring you prosperity.

#33 Be a Builder, Not a Bomber

"Keep away from people who belittle your ambitions. Small people always do that, but the really great make you feel that you, too, can become great."

MARK TWAIN

As you go about your daily activities, be a builder of people. Be an encourager to those around you on a regular basis. You will only be "new" in the business until the next training class is complete, then you are suddenly the more experienced one. Always remember how it feels to be brand new at something. When the next group completes their training be sure to offer an encouraging word, share a comical experience or pass on something meaningful you may have heard.

The business is tough, competitive and riddled with rejection. Don't add to it in the office. Agents come back into the office to emotionally refuel, to connect with others who understand how the marketplace works and to share their experiences from the day. Never underestimate the impact of a simple gesture, a kind word or a pat on the back. Your casual comment may keep someone from quitting or encourage them to get back at it.

When you consciously become a builder and encourager, you not only lift up others but also strengthen your own convictions and fortify your own attitude. This doesn't mean you are always a cheerleader; there are times when constructive criticism is warranted, but even that can be delivered in a caring way.

Practicing this behavior in the office will also help you to make it a habit with your clients and prospects. Look for the good in people and help them see what they can become. Remember the adage, "People don't care how much you know until they know how much you care."

#34 Pay Your Dues Now or Pay Them Later

"Nothing happens by itself...it all will come your way once you understand that you have to make it come your way, by your own exertions."

BEN STEIN

One of the natural laws of business is that you have to pay your dues to succeed. You can pay them now or pay them later, but there's no way around paying them.

You can accelerate your success in the first year through sustained high activity early on. Or you can struggle in the later years, doomed to repeat your first year again and again because you spent too much time savoring the flexibility you hadn't yet earned and not enough time working.

Think of what paying dues literally means: sacrificing something today to gain a benefit in the future. Paying dues to a club or organization means you sacrifice financially to reap the benefit of the club's resources. Paying dues in this business means you work some evenings and weekends early in your career and give up a few rounds of golf or other activities so that you can play at your leisure in future years. It means occasionally turning down your friends who want to socialize during the week because you have early morning appointments and want to be sharp. It means meeting with people who won't buy from you, meeting people who are financially irresponsible, having policies declined in underwriting, having people change their minds after they've bought and so on.

If you aren't willing to endure these things then you will never appreciate how good the business can be. You can either have the pain of discipline today or the pain of regret tomorrow. If you choose wisely, you will build a strong business and an even stronger character.

#35 Reflect Before You Reject

"The best way to get a good idea is to get a lot of ideas."
LINUS PAULING

Be careful not to be more committed to being right than to being successful. Often people are so committed to their way of thinking they don't let any new ideas creep in. In fact, they vigilantly stand guard against anything that doesn't fit in with what they already know or believe. Don't forget, there was a large contingent of people who at one time thought with great conviction that the world was flat.

When new information comes your way, pause, listen carefully and give it some thought. You don't have to revise your belief system every five minutes, but it's wise to carefully consider new information before accepting or rejecting it. When someone gives you a new sales idea or technique and it's radically different from what you thought you knew, ponder it before you decide it's a crazy idea.

What does it cost you to listen and process an idea before rejecting it? There are several things to consider: What is the source of the information? Is it reliable? Has the person advocating the idea ever used it successfully? Have you heard it before? If you are able to answer yes to these queries, then perhaps the information deserves your attention.

Some ideas have withstood the test of time; others are no more than a passing fad. But you will never know which is which if you are so committed to your current way of thinking that new ideas are turned away at the gate before a thorough inspection.

Being receptive doesn't mean you let every new idea take root; it simply means that you reflect before you reject or accept.

#36 Mirror, Mirror on the Wall

"A loving person lives in a loving world. A hostile person lives in a hostile world. Everyone you meet is your mirror."

KEN KEYS

The marketplace you are about to enter is a mirror that reflects exactly who you are (enter "Twilight Zone" music.) Let's focus on one specific concept in this area: The excuses you make for yourself are likely to be the same excuses you will hear and tolerate from your prospects and clients.

Think about this: If you haven't bought any of your own products because you have too much credit card debt, then how will you respond when a prospect defers buying from you for the same reason? If you are lax about keeping your own commitments, how can you expect prospects and clients to keep their appointments with you?

Brian, an enthusiastic new agent, was having a terrible time with cancellations. He tried making more appointments, confirming each appointment and rescheduling cancelled appointments, but nothing seemed to work. About 75 percent of his appointments routinely cancelled. Upon closer examination, it turns out that Brian wasn't too diligent about things like taking out the trash when he said he would, walking the dog when he said he would or helping his wife at home when he said he would. He didn't believe there was a connection – after all, he said, how could my prospects possibly know any of those things? He didn't want to look in the marketplace mirror. He left the business within six months.

When you repeatedly hear the same excuses or have the same struggles, always look in the mirror first to see what adjustments need to be made in your situation before judging others too quickly.

#37 Activity Trumps Brains

"You can impress people at a distance, but you can impact them only up close."

HOWARD HENDRICKS

It will be tempting in your early days to stock up on knowledge to the exclusion of activity. You will tell yourself that you need to study more so that you will bring more value to people. You'll be tempted to take days out of the business to work on the Series 6, 63, 7, 9, 10 or whatever other test you have chosen, believing that these accomplishments will in and of themselves raise your business to a higher level.

While it is important to become technically proficient in your business, it cannot take the place of being face to face with people. You will learn enough in your licensing process and initial training to know more than the majority of the marketplace. Simply learning the difference between term and permanent insurance puts you ahead of some of the most successful people you will meet. Remember, this is your chosen field, not theirs.

Your business will grow because you see enough people to generate sales. All of the additional education will help the size and scope of some of your cases, but passing a test will not by itself generate more business. It doesn't matter how smart you are, everyone you see will not buy from you. There are people with no more than their initial licenses who are members of the Million Dollar Round Table, and people who have an entire alphabet of letters behind their names who are struggling to make ends meet.

It isn't an "either-or" proposition – you need both education and activity to grow a successful business. But in your initial days and months, it is far more important to focus on your activity. You have an entire career to amass your credentials – you only have one chance to build your foundation.

#38 Structure Equals Freedom

"Disciplining yourself to do what you know is right and important, although difficult, is the high road to pride, self-esteem and personal satisfaction."

BRIAN TRACY

Structure, routine, discipline and habits are critical to your long-term success. There are certain things you know you have to do every day. Developing a structure or set of habits that you can overlay on each day makes the big picture less intimidating.

Freedom is the most popular reason for entering this business. Ironically, the only way to attain that freedom is to develop structure and daily discipline. You know you have to make a certain number of daily phone calls – why not make them at the same time every day? You know you have to record your activities and results for the day – why not do it at the same time every day? When you allot specific times for specific activities, there is a much greater chance that you will get them done.

Waiting until you magically have time to do something, particularly something difficult, is a sure way not to get it done. Unassigned time has a way of slipping by unnoticed until it's too late. Looking at your calendar and knowing exactly when you will be phoning, seeing people, exercising or any other activity leaves your brain free to work on more important things. You don't have to constantly make decisions every few minutes about where you can fit things in.

Imagine trying to drive somewhere without a system of roads to keep you on track. Even a detour is manageable because there is a specific structure to follow. Naturally there will be times when things don't flow exactly as you had planned. But if you have an order and structure to each day, it's much easier to deal with the unexpected.

#39 Understand and Appreciate Everyone

"People must believe in each other and feel that it can be done and it must be done; in that way they are enormously strong. We must keep up each other's courage."
VINCENT VAN GOGH

Compassion is a trait that you must develop to keep your sanity in this business. People will stand you up, let you down, break your heart, hang up on you, ignore your advice, rescind their decisions, buy from someone else and argue with you until they are blue in the face. To keep from throwing things at them, you must see them through compassionate eyes. Remember they are human beings just like you and they have their idiosyncrasies, just like you.

Compassion is also a sign of wisdom and maturity. You have to realize in a business like this one that you are dealing with people and their behaviors and emotions. To you, it may look and sound perfectly logical, but keep in mind that people buy on emotion, not logic. They may justify the purchase with logic, but it is seldom why they bought in the first place. People also don't buy because you dazzled them with a brilliant presentation. In reality, most people just want to know the time, not how the watch works.

Compassion doesn't mean necessarily agreeing with people all the time; it means understanding and appreciating their position while sticking to your guns. It is a great human need to be understood, and if your prospects and clients feel that you understand them, even if you don't agree with them, they will respect you and stick with you over your career. Your ability to peacefully and consistently go forward, sticking to your position while exhibiting kindness and compassion for others, will yield astounding results.

#40 Busy as a Bee (or a Mosquito)

"It is not so much how busy you are – but why you are busy. The bee is praised. The mosquito is swatted."

MARIE O'CONNOR

Most people live at the mercy of their day and whatever occurs in it. They will tell you that they had the best of intentions, but the day "just got away." The same people will also tell you that they have a vision of their "ideal" day, but that it's just not practical – after all, they can't control what happens in the day, right?

Seldom will you have a day in which something unexpected doesn't happen. But, seldom will an unexpected event carry the power to destroy an entire day. And even if it happens occasionally, it isn't going to happen every day.

Stick to the idea that you can influence the day's events from start to finish. Plan your ideal day and work on making it happen daily. When you make a commitment, don't dilute it by saying "Well, it depends on how the day goes." How the day goes depends entirely on you.

People go wrong by writing off an entire day when one little thing doesn't go just right. Their justification is "I'll just start again tomorrow" when, in fact, the day is far from over and progress could still be made, even in small increments.

Your "ideal" day provides the framework to keep you on track toward your goals. It's not about living the perfect day every day. It's about never giving up when there is still mileage left in the day.

#41 The Phone Is Your Friend

"Most of our obstacles would melt away if, instead of cowering before them, we should make up our minds to walk boldly through them."

ORISON SWETT MARDEN

You will at some point come to think of the telephone as the enemy. It happens to everyone. Even the veteran producers will tell you they don't like to call on new people. It's hard, it's scary, and it's absolutely vital to your success. If you can't muster the courage to make the phone calls, you will fail. There is no way to cushion the blow on this one. New agents have creatively tried to avoid the phone to no avail. Learn to love the telephone, or prepare to do battle with it for the rest of your career.

It isn't the actual phone – let's face it, the phone is an inanimate object with no power to harm you. It's the person at the other end of the phone who's just sitting there waiting for you to call so they can say "no" to you. Most new agents find calling early in the day and getting it over with helps them deal with the fear of phoning. Building it right into your calendar as its own appointment is a must for many. Make a game of it or have a contest with another new agent to see who can get their calls for the day done the fastest. Teaming up makes this task more manageable.

Don't wait until the end of the day to do most of your phoning – you will have then saved the hardest part of your day for last when you will be tired and likely to come up with excuses. Doing it early will be a huge relief and will get you fired up for the rest of your day.

The science of the numbers indicates that at least some of the people you call will say "yes." That's just a fact. The other fact is that almost all of them will say "no" at least once before you get to that magical "yes." So, be prepared to overcome at least one objection in every call. This is where having your language memorized and at your fingertips will give you confidence. There are about eight to 10 basic objections and once you have language to overcome them you are on your way.

Don't let the phone get the best of you. Tame it into submission, and turn it into the moneymaker it was meant to be.

#42 Get Paid for Your Time

"Perseverance is the hard work you do after you get tired of doing the hard work you already did."

NEWT GINGRICH

The other power "P" that goes hand-in-hand with phoning is prospecting. You must become a master prospector if you want to build a successful business. Some agents tend to look at prospecting as begging for help. You have to change that outlook. After all, you are as professional as an attorney, an accountant or a doctor, and you deserve to get paid for your time just as they do. You just get paid a little differently, that's all.

Being introduced is much easier than introducing yourself. This is the difference between referred leads and cold calls. The more relaxed you are about asking, the more relaxed your prospect or client will be with the process. Process is the key word here – if you can train yourself to ask at least twice a day for prospects, you will be surprised at how many names you will receive over time. Expect to average about two names per time asked. It's a science just like the other activities involved in the business. Some people will give you one or two names, some will give you five or six names, and some will not give you any names. In the end, if it averages out to two names per time asked, you are doing a good job.

Unfortunately, you don't know who will give referred leads and who won't, so you must develop the habit of asking without judgment. You can always choose not to call a referred lead you received – you can't get a referred lead you didn't ask for. The other benefit of asking everyone is that you train your clients and prospects to expect you to ask every time you see them. After a while they may even have leads ready for you, knowing that you will ask. As you build your business through referred leads, there will come a time when your clients may even call you with a referred lead before you ask. That's when you know you have arrived.

#43 You Have to Kiss a Lot of Frogs

"When I was a young man, I observed that nine out of the ten things I did were failures. Not wanting to be a failure, I did ten times more work."

THEODORE ROOSEVELT

Don't be too judgmental in the beginning. You will meet with many prospects early in your career that you won't necessarily want to have as clients. Think of this as part of paying your dues. Unfortunately, the prospects who will become good clients aren't marked with a special sign so you won't always recognize them at first.

A top producer tells the story of arriving at a rundown office in a seedy section of town early in his career. As he went inside he became more depressed because the office was simply a metal desk and a beat-up file cabinet. After the prospect introduced himself, he asked the agent if he wanted to go out back and see what he did for a living. As it turned out, the prospect owned the largest earth-moving machinery business in the state. He went on to become a good client.

Another agent tells of a time she was having lunch with a client. After the client left, the waitress asked the agent if she was in the financial services business because the waitress had just inherited some money and wanted to invest it wisely. She would not have necessarily been viewed as a desirable prospect.

On the other hand, a young agent talks about meeting with a prospect who didn't have much income or much potential for that matter. But he went to the meeting because he understood the nature of paying dues. During the factfinding process the agent asked for some financial investment information, including whether the prospect had any C.D.s, to which the prospect replied, "Sure, I have lots – what do you want to listen to?"

You can't afford to be too judgmental in the early months of your career. Meet everyone because you don't know what's under the surface. Sure, you will find a few disappointments, but you might also uncover a few surprises that make it all worthwhile.

#44 Don't Pre-judge

"We probably wouldn't worry about what people think of us if we could know how seldom they do."

OLIN MILLER

As you get started in your career, you can't be too particular about who you are and aren't willing to meet. Obviously, not having a job or a place to live are criteria that might take someone off the list of potential prospects, but otherwise meet everyone you can. Some will be great prospects and some will not. Until you meet with them, you won't necessarily be able to tell. Don't underestimate whom someone might know – just because a person isn't your ideal prospect keep in mind that they could have a relative, neighbor or other acquaintance who might be just the person for whom you are looking.

Ask everyone for referrals without regard to their situation in life – the janitor's brother-in-law might be a cardiac surgeon. You can always weed people out later, but you can't weed out what you don't have. Every agent wants to upgrade his or her market. There's nothing wrong with aspiring to get in front of people who can write bigger checks, but in the beginning, unless you already have connections to those kinds of people, you will have to work your way up.

Good prospects can come from unlikely sources. While it's true that people will most likely refer you to others who are similar to them, every now and then you will be surprised by a referral to someone's boss or the owner of the business. Remember that the more specific you are about what you want, the more likely you are to get it. If you define your "ideal" prospect and ask for that type of person, you are much more likely to have success in building your business with the kinds of people you enjoy being around.

#45 Priming the Pump

"There is no point at which you can say, "Well, I'm successful now. I might as well take a nap."

CARRIE FISHER

A large part of your success will depend on your willingness to continue calling on new people. In the first six months, this happens naturally because you are starting from scratch and don't have any base for repeat business. After that, it becomes easier to rely on repeat sales from existing clients. Repeat sales are a wonderful thing, and you should strive to have as many as possible, but keep in mind that eventually the last person buys for the last time and then the compounding of your business comes to a screeching halt.

In the first year, at least 70 percent of your sales should be to new people. Therefore, if you sold 100 policies in year one, then 70 of them should be new. Think of "new" as a new-paying entity. In other words, if you sold policies on a family of five, it is likely that only one person is paying the entire premium for all the policies, so although it may be five policies it is only one paying entity.

Statistics indicate that a client will purchase from you on average at least five to seven more times. It stands to reason that the more new people you add to your client base, the more repeat sales you are accumulating for the future.

The more difficult the activity, typically the greater the rewards associated with it. An agent at any stage of the business finds calling new people a challenge. The disciplined few will do it anyway and build powerful, sustainable businesses.

#46 Record and Review

"Make it a point to do something every day that you don't want to do. This is the golden rule for acquiring the habit of doing your duty without pain."

MARK TWAIN

Although seeing people and phoning to see people are two of the most important aspects of this business, they aren't the only things that need to be done. Part of the daily discipline of long-term success is keeping thorough and accurate records.

This is probably the least glamorous and most tedious part of any given day. But think about this: The owner of an electronics store wouldn't just throw open the doors each day without knowing exactly what was on the shelves and what was in the storeroom. Nor would she close the store at the end of the day without some record of exactly what was sold, what needed to be restocked and how much sales revenue was produced. The only difference in your business is that what you sell is not tangible like a stereo or a television.

You still have an inventory that you need to track (prospects, factfinders, open cases) and you still have to monitor results (closing attempts, sales.) Failure to do this on a daily basis will put you among the 95 percent of small businesses that fail within the first few years. You cannot operate a successful business without keeping records; to attempt to do so is wishful thinking.

An excellent record-keeping resource is O. Alfred Granum's book *Building a Financial Services Clientele*. This is a proven method of tracking activity and results specifically for this industry.

Keeping daily records is part of being a professional. Don't hide from it because you had a bad day. Agents who don't keep records typically don't have good activity or results. They mistakenly think if they don't write it down, it can't really be happening or that no one will know. In reality, this discipline will make both you and your business rock solid.

#47 Read to Lead

"The only two things that will make you a different person five years from now are the books you read and the people you are around."
CHARLIE "TREMENDOUS" JONES

Reading for some people is pure pleasure and for others it's sheer torture. Regardless of which reaction you have, it's a fact that if you are going to develop yourself, you need a steady diet of new information. For those who don't enjoy reading, lots of excuses are probably popping into your head right now. "I don't have time," "I hate to read," "It's too expensive." Banish those thoughts. Realize that there is more than one way to get information from a book. Most popular books can be found in audio format. Airline magazine ads tout "Executive Book Summaries," concise summaries of the latest business books for time-deprived readers.

For those who love to read, the challenge is usually switching from fiction to non-fiction. This doesn't mean you can't ever read a Tom Clancy or Sue Grafton novel again. It means expanding your repertoire. You can still have dessert, you just have to add a vegetable.

The printed word can inspire, inform, educate, encourage and literally change the way you look at the world and the people in it. The best performers in any industry will tell you that they study continuously in order to better serve their clients and stay ahead of the competition.

A book won't change your life just from the reading of it. It's putting the ideas into action that changes things. You can speed your way through 12 books, check them off a list and proudly announce that you did it, but what did you gain? Read as though you had to teach the material to others because, whether you realize it or not, that's exactly what you are doing with your clients and peers.

#48 Like Attracts Like

"Excellence is not an event, it is a habit. You are what you repeatedly do."

ARISTOTLE

As you go about meeting anyone and everyone, you will develop an idea of whom you deem to be your "ideal" prospect. Just like with your goals, the more details you can ascribe to these people, the more likely you are to find them. Keeping in mind that "like attracts like," you will find yourself taking on the characteristics of your "ideal" in order to attract them as prospects.

Remember that character traits are equally, if not more important in describing prospects than income ranges or professions. There are plenty of high-income people in prestigious professions who are irresponsible, uncaring or living well beyond their means, and there are plenty of middle-income people who are diligently saving money. You have only to read any of Thomas Stanley's books on millionaires to see that who you think they are and who they really are is quite different.

Once you have a clear picture in your mind and on paper of whom you would like to work with, begin asking specifically for that person when you prospect. Remember, you will obtain these quality referred leads as you get better yourself. You are seeking quality and quantity – one does not absolve you of the responsibility for the other. Quality and quantity are not mutually exclusive. Having only a few of the kind of people you want to see is a start but remember that not all of them will see you, and of those who do agree to see you, not all of them will buy from you. Only when you have both quantity and quality will you begin to see a change in your business.

#49 To Get Better Prospects – Become One

"Most people want to change the world to improve their lives. What a wasted effort. If they would only improve themselves, they would be better off and so would the world."

AUTHOR UNKNOWN

If you've hit a wall in any aspect of your business, chances are good that you are looking externally for solutions that can usually be found internally. Take prospecting, for example. Most new agents want to get in front of "better" prospects, those who make more money, are more responsible or have a higher net worth.

So the logical question is "How can I get in front of better prospects?" New agents spend lots of time learning new prospecting language, seeking new techniques for networking, defining their ideal prospect and judging everyone in terms of how they fit the ideal. These are all necessary activities to improve prospecting, but only if the real question has been addressed first: not "How can I get in front of better prospects?" but "Whom do I have to become to deserve to be in front of better prospects?"

When you are banging your head against the proverbial brick wall because the marketplace isn't responding the way you want it to, look internally before you drown yourself in new ideas and techniques. Remember, the marketplace is a mirror reflecting yourself back to you. If you want prospects who will save more money, you must first save more money yourself. If you want more responsible prospects, you must first become more responsible yourself. People are drawn to those who are most like themselves, so you must mold yourself to become more like the prospect you wish to attract.

If you will develop the habit of looking inside yourself first before frantically changing the external factors, you will save time and energy. Making small adjustments internally will ultimately yield bigger results than making big adjustments externally.

#50 Turn Anxiety into Adrenaline

"The problems of the world cannot possibly be solved by skeptics or cynics whose horizons are limited by the obvious realities. We need people who can dream of things that never were."

JOHN F. KENNEDY

From the moment you signed up for this career you have probably had battalions of butterflies in your stomach. Some people feel this anxiety and work harder; others become paralyzed by it. Turn your anxiety into adrenaline and join the group who works harder. Quit fighting fear and make it your partner. Some measure of fear, anxiety, stress or whatever you want to call it is necessary to push you forward.

Even experienced producers feel some anxiety on a regular basis. They use it to propel themselves to the next level. Fear will grow or shrink in proportion to how much you dwell on it. Action helps reduce fear to a manageable size – inaction makes it grow larger. The downward spiral occurs as you sit alone thinking at length about the fears you have. Jumping into action, whether that means making some phone calls or talking it through with someone, can make a huge difference. Sometimes just giving voice to the fear can shrink it down to size.

Make sure when you talk to someone, it's someone who's doing well. Don't get together with another agent who is also quaking with fear; that only results in everyone feeling worse. You can always find someone who will feel sorry for you – what you need in the midst of fear is someone who will listen for a few minutes, give you some encouragement and then tell you to get back to work.

#51 Hard Work Beats Talent

"Getting ahead in a difficult profession requires avid faith in yourself. That is why some people with mediocre talent, but with great inner drive, go much further than people with vastly superior talent."

SOPHIA LOREN

Talent is only worthwhile when it goes hand-in-hand with hard work. An agent of average talent who sees an abundance of people in the beginning will, over time, build a more valuable business than an agent of tremendous talent who sees only a chosen few. It is tempting to think that you can hone your skills to the point that everyone who sees you will buy from you, and therefore you can get by seeing less people. This will not happen. *Repeat, this will not happen.*

In the beginning you will have to see lots of people. In fact, to build a solid foundation for future years, you will want to see 15 to 20 people per week. If you have average talent but see this many people, you will get better by sheer repetition. You will also enhance your chances of "stumbling" onto some unexpected opportunities. If you have tremendous talent and see this many people, you will be off to such a fast start it will make your head spin. However, if you have tremendous talent but only see eight to 10 people per week, you will eventually struggle.

Talent alone will not propel you to fame or financial freedom. As you have probably read more than once, the world is full of people not living up to their potential or squandering their talents. Just because you have a business degree, graduated at the top of your class or know a lot of wealthy people, you will still need to work hard every single day in the early years.

#52 Defy Gravity

"People say motivation doesn't last. Well, neither does bathing – that's why we recommend it daily."

ZIG ZIGLAR

Gravity is a natural law that pulls you downward and keeps you attached to the earth. In fact, it takes a rocket blast to get you far enough away from the earth to detach from gravity. Some people can be like that also. At least half of the people you meet on a daily basis are like gravity: It seems like their purpose, whether intentional or not, is to pull you down. They constantly rain on your parade by belittling your ideas, pointing out why things won't work, reminding you of past failures, whining, complaining and just generally wanting to share their misery.

To battle emotional gravity you must deliberately seek out people who are like rockets: They lift you from the forces of gravity and shore up your energy and enthusiasm. You know these people when you meet them; they exude energy and a positive aura. They get as excited about your ideas as you do and cheer rather than envy your accomplishments. When you can't find these rocket-booster people, you can get similar results by reading positive, inspirational and informative material daily. That way you create a storehouse of positive ideas that act as a vaccine against the inevitable parade of gravity grubbers.

You can't avoid the people who pull you down; there are too many of them. Some will probably even become your clients. The best you can do is to recognize them, feel compassion for them and make sure you are equipped to shake off the results of your encounters with them.

#53 Mental Toughness Training Camp

"Little minds are tamed and subdued by misfortune; great minds rise above them."

WASHINGTON IRVING

Your mental toughness will be tested often as you build your career, especially in the first year because everything is unfamiliar. Think of it as mental toughness training camp. People will disappoint you, cases you thought would go won't, people you thought would give you referred leads don't, and you will doubt yourself more than times than you can count. Sounds like great fun, right?

Don't worry; everyone gets tested – that's just part of the growth process. You may feel like you are the only one who has ever entertained thoughts of quitting, but most veteran agents will tell you they thought about it daily in the beginning. It's like fighting a battle. When things are toughest, the temptation to retreat and retrench is the highest. But if you can keep charging forward through the adversity, you will win the battle. Then the next time adversity strikes, you will have more confidence because you made it through last time and you know you will again.

Once you get to the other side of adversity, you can look back and realize that you survived intact, unharmed and a little wiser. If you develop the habit of retreating every time the going gets tough, the obstacle will loom even larger next time because you haven't faced it down yet.

Force yourself to stretch and grow to meet the challenges that will present themselves and you will beat the odds and have a long, prosperous career. Don't wait – training camp starts right now!

#54 Thank You, Sir, May I Have Another?

"Perseverance is not a long race. It is many short races one after another."

WALTER ELLIOTT

One of the most frustrating experiences new agents have is the continual stream of "no's" that they hear in the course of doing business. Here is something that you must understand from the beginning – you will always hear more of the word "no" than you will ever hear of the word "yes."

You may have the best company, the best product, the best approach, the best close, or all of the above, but there will always be more people who do not buy than do. Many new agents spend lots of time trying to minimize the "no" by perfecting their language, gaining more technical knowledge, seeking the ideal prospect and so forth. These are all beneficial activities that will help your business, but none of them will make the "no" disappear.

Unfortunately, you cannot tell just by looking at your prospects which ones will say "no" and which ones will say "yes." Those who aren't going to buy from you do not walk around with a big, red "X" on their forehead. Of course, it would be much simpler if they did. Then you could eliminate them right away. Instead, you have to meet with a large number of human beings to get to the few who are going to buy from you. Those who truly understand this business and succeed at it accept this fact early in their careers.

No matter how good you are, not everyone will buy from you. Repeat, not everyone will buy from you. You are dealing with human beings and their emotions which rarely conform to logic. Those who can fortify themselves to withstand the onslaught of "no's" will ultimately rise to the top of their professions.

"What you do speaks so loudly that I cannot hear what you say."

RALPH WALDO EMERSON

An accepted rule of thumb in the financial services business is this: You will sell to others monthly approximately what you pay annually for the products you own. Let's use life insurance products as an example. If you pay $5,000 of annual premium for your policies, you will sell roughly $5,000 of premium per month. Test this idea on some of the successful agents you know. Check the published reports to see what they are selling monthly, and ask if they will share the details of what they own. Those who are proud of what they own usually won't hesitate to tell you.

Your willingness to own a significant amount of your product demonstrates to others your deep belief in it. Why would someone buy a large amount of any product when the person selling it either does not own it at all or only owns a small amount of it? So, it stands to reason that if you want to sell more, you must own more. Be careful about the excuses you make for not owning more; they are likely to be the same excuses your prospects make for not buying from you.

Those who have achieved significant success in the financial services field are constantly updating their own financial situation with the products they sell. What you do is much more significant than what you say. You must "walk the talk."

#56 Cover the Need

"If you limit your actions in life to things that nobody can possibly find fault with, you will not do much."

LEWIS CARROLL

People die or become uninsurable every day at every age. No one thinks it will happen to them, but day after day it does. You must do the right thing for your clients regarding their life insurance needs. Develop your philosophy about insurance products and their place in people's overall financial picture. Your prospects and clients look to you as the expert so you must be prepared to share your beliefs in a convincing manner. Finding their insurance needs through complete factfinding interviews will help your clients see, through mutual discovery, what they need to do. People often have negative, preconceived ideas about insurance which you will have to overcome. (Remember, this stuff has to be sold.)

Covering a client's total insurance need is more important than the specific products used. A combination of term and permanent life insurance to cover a need is better than a smaller whole life policy that only solves part of the problem. Developing a trusting relationship begins when your prospects and clients believe that you are truly there to solve their needs and problems, not just to make a big commission.

Again, what you own and how it relates to your specific situation is more convincing than any theory you may have developed about what other people should be doing. You can always convert term insurance to permanent insurance down the road. If someone dies or becomes uninsurable, you can't go back and fix the fact that you didn't cover the need.

#57 Earn While You Learn

"There is no such thing as "them and us." In a world this size there can only be "we" – all of us working together."

DON WARD

A popular success theory says you should watch and mimic the experts in your field. This means inviting a willing veteran performer to join you on some of your calls. This practice of "joint work" also means being willing to share the commission if a sale is made. Most new agents are more than willing to execute the first part of that equation, but balk at the second.

Most hesitation stems from fear of giving up income. The thought of having to share any of your commissions may freeze you in your tracks. You will probably wonder daily "Am I going to be able to pay the bills?" when taking on the challenge of this commission-based endeavor. Unless you reframe this thinking process, you are wasting one of your most valuable resources.

A veteran agent's wisdom, experience and expertise may yield results where your own efforts did not. An abundant mentality is a must – after all, 50 percent of something is better than 100 percent of nothing. Think of it as tuition for a master class. Bringing in an expert may yield much bigger results so that your 50 percent of a case could be greater than the 100 percent you would have obtained on your own. On the other hand, bringing in a veteran does not guarantee results. The science still applies. Not everyone will buy from you regardless of who is involved, but you can still learn a great deal.

Your attitude about doing joint work will have a measurable impact on your success. Use all of your available resources – the lessons you learn at a master's hand will serve you well for years to come.

#58 Tap the Well of Knowledge

"As a kid I learned that my brother and I could walk forever on a railroad track and never fall off – if we just reached across the track and held each other's hands."

STEVE POTTER

As you meet the veteran agents in your company's office, develop relationships with them. These are the people who have traveled the path before you and are fountains of wisdom and knowledge. Usually, they are willing to share their experiences with you and occasionally may go on joint appointments with you. They will help you understand the business through the eyes of experience.

Find someone who has built a successful business and ask them to mentor you. Veteran agents are usually generous with their time and knowledge. They remember how difficult it was to get started and are usually happy to help and encourage you. The advantage to the veteran is the possibility of increased income through joint work, the ability to develop a protégée or successor in the business and the good feeling that comes from giving something back in a career that has been extremely rewarding.

While you are cultivating relationships with veteran agents, be careful not to waste their time with idle chatter. Have a purpose or a specific question, and don't take it personally if, on occasion, they don't have time to talk. Just because they are established doesn't mean they don't work hard. Even veteran agents are still growing their businesses and taking on new challenges.

Demonstrate your seriousness about building your business by keeping your activity high and working hard. Veteran agents will be more likely to spend time with you if they see tangible evidence that you are in the business for the long term.

#59 Should I Stay or Should I Go?

"Many of life's failures are people who did not realize how close they were to success when they gave up."
THOMAS EDISON

There will be times when you feel like you have hit rock bottom. Times when you just can't see the light at the end of the tunnel and you decide that you are going to leave the business. These are not the times to make life-altering decisions.

It's unwise to make decisions when you are at the height of your emotions, or based on temporary circumstances. For example, before you make the decision that you are going to leave the business, take a good look at what triggered that notion. Are you fearful because you don't know where your next check is coming from? Did you just experience a commission reversal? Another close with no sale? No one is giving you referred leads? In the early days in particular, you will be tempted to leave the business numerous times as these inevitable things occur. It will seem like the sane and reasonable solution at the time.

But, before you make the decision to quit, ask yourself, "Is this set of circumstances temporary or permanent?" Make sure you are making decisions based on facts as well as emotions. Both components are important in your decision-making process.

Ask yourself, "What will be the consequences of this decision five years from now?" Then talk to a veteran agent who will assure you that everyone lives through the "Should I stay or should I go?" dilemma numerous times in the early stages. Here's the reality: You have little control over the doubts that inevitably will surface, but you have complete control over how long they linger.

Keep in mind that few people leave the business when it's going well. If you really believe you want to quit, then make sure it's for the right reasons.

#60 Seek What You Need

"Parties who want milk should not seat themselves on a stool in the middle of a field in hope that the cow will back up to them."

ELBERT HUBBARD

Successful people seek what they need when they need it. They don't wait for someone to show them the way or blame someone else for not providing resources. Everyone will receive a certain amount of training in the beginning. Some companies have better training programs than others. Yet, there are successful agents from all sorts of companies. You have only to attend a Million Dollar Round Table meeting to see that one company doesn't have a monopoly on top-producing agents.

One of the common characteristics of these top-producing agents is that they don't wait to be spoon-fed. They are proactive in marshalling their resources and making good use of everything at their disposal. New product lines have been created because good agents recognized a need in the marketplace and brought it to the attention of their companies. They didn't sit around waiting for their companies to come up with the ideas.

If you need a mentor, seek one out. Don't wait for someone to come to you and offer to help. Read on your own – don't wait for a reading assignment. Your success to a large degree will depend on your ability to find and use resources beyond what those presented to you.

Developing the habit of seeking out what you need to succeed will enrich all aspects of your life, not just your business. It will separate you from the victims and whiners of the world who wait to be given the magic ingredients for success and then blame and complain when no such thing appears.

#61 All Work and No Play

"Every now and then go away, have a little relaxation, for when you come back to your work your judgment will be surer."

LEONARDO DA VINCI

A business driven by the concept that you only get paid when you work tends to make you feel like you should work all the time. It's easy to justify spending 12 to 15 hours a day six or seven days a week working in the early days and totally neglecting the rest of your life. The problem is that this becomes a habit that's difficult to break later on. It may sound contradictory to say work hard, but don't spend all your time working. However, if you want to have a full life you have to tend to all aspects of it. The emphasis may shift from personal to business and back again with regularity.

Think about it this way: If you are working all the time there is still a part of your brain that is thinking about the fact that you have no free time, you haven't exercised in days, you haven't seen your kids awake in weeks, or you haven't read a book in months. It becomes a snowball effect that saps energy from both your business and your personal life.

It's true you have to make some sacrifices early on – maybe the family vacation waits another year or you skip a year with theater tickets, but staying connected to your family and friends is vital to your success. If you are single, it's still important to create a full life for yourself – it makes you more interesting to your prospects and clients.

Take some of your evenings and weekends to relax and enjoy what you are building. It won't result in your business falling apart as long as you are focused and doing the right job when you are working.

#62 What You Need to Hear

"It's very easy to forgive others their mistakes, it takes more gut and gumption to forgive them for having witnessed your own."

JESSAMYN WEST

As you enter the financial services business you are wise to affiliate with a company that supports you through ups and downs and helps you grow. Support doesn't mean that your peers, those on the staff or in management tell you how wonderful you are all the time. It means they care enough to give you an honest assessment of your strengths and challenges. They tell you what you need to hear, which is not always what you want to hear.

As you go through life, you develop blind spots about yourself where you can't or don't want to see certain issues. It often takes an outside source to point out what you might not be aware of. It is only from these encounters that you grow and change. If people are only telling you the good stuff why would you ever change or grow? What can you learn when everything is going great? It feels good and there's nothing wrong with positive feedback, but there's no incentive to change anything when the perception is that all is well.

When feedback is given in a tone of caring and commitment, it provides the impetus for development. It's a two-way responsibility – you want to provide feedback to those around you as well to encourage their development. This is not an easy task and takes practice. If you can develop the habit of doing this with your peers, prospects, clients, family and friends, they will regard you with respect as someone to consult on major decisions.

#63 School's Never Out of Session

"Unless you try to do something beyond what you have already mastered, you will never grow."
RALPH WALDO EMERSON

After you have established your ability to stick with this business for at least a year, you should begin pursuing one of the professional designations available to you such as Chartered Life Underwriter (CLU), Chartered Financial Consultant (ChFC) or Certified Financial Planner (CFP), among others. Professional designations indicate that you have studied in your field and that you care about expanding your base of knowledge to benefit your clients.

These designations also indicate to your prospects and clients that you are up-to-date regarding the technical aspects of your field. People will know you cared enough to study further even if they don't know what the specific letters stand for. Imagine you are buying a house and two realtors present you with cards. One simply has a name on it, the other has a name with two professional designations after it – with whom are you more likely to do business?

This is not to say that designations alone will magically increase your business. If you don't have the other elements of hard work, discipline and high activity, these designations will merely make you a very smart failure. That's why it's important to have at least a year under your belt before you begin these rigorous courses of study. You need to focus on building your business then layer your studies on top of that.

As with most things in life, the benefits of pursuing advanced studies are two-fold – the knowledge you gain will help you increase your ability to help people and lead to larger cases, and the discipline required to start and finish will increase your self-confidence and further develop your character.

#64 Join the Cream of the Crop

"Success is to be measured not so much by the position that one has reached in life as by the obstacles which he has overcome while trying to succeed."
BOOKER T. WASHINGTON

Qualifying for the Million Dollar Round Table (MDRT) is a professional distinction that less than 10 percent of the world's top producers achieve annually. MDRT is an organization committed to the growth and professionalism of financial services professionals around the world. It has set the standard for the industry and has done more to establish credibility and professionalism than any other organization. It hosts what is widely considered the best annual sales meetings in the world, with speakers including Rudy Guiliani, Colin Powell, Ronin Tynan and Liz Murray.

Some veteran agents will tell you that it is worth the effort to qualify just to attend these annual meetings. Qualification is difficult and measured by attaining either a premium or first-year commission requirement that increases each year. The requirement is the same across the industry regardless of company affiliation. It is unusual but not impossible to qualify for this elite organization in your first year. Once you have qualified the first time, you will never want to miss a year. A common standard is qualification by your fourth year in the business.

Qualification for MDRT signifies your commitment to professionalism and a high-caliber business. Attending the meetings gives you the opportunity to meet your peers from around the world. You will see that high producers come from many different backgrounds and countries. Most people come back fully charged and committed to never missing a year of qualification.

Qualification also provides you with benefits and resources not available to non-qualifying producers. It is just one of the ways that you can mark significant progress in your career. Remember, though, it is best to qualify through consistent activity and high lives production.

#65 Little Daily Decisions

"The reason most people never reach their goals is that they don't define them, or ever seriously consider them as believable or achievable."

DENIS WAITLEY

Goals give purpose to the daily grind. If you don't have specific, measurable goals then you are engaged in wishful thinking, not business-building. Without goals, every setback looms larger, every failure seems fatal. When you are focused on a specific outcome, it is much easier to push through the inevitable obstacles.

Having goals in your head is not the same as writing them down. The act of writing a goal on paper brings it one step closer to reality. Going public brings it closer still. When you share your goals with others, you build in powerful accountability.

You will also begin to see that it is truly the little, daily decisions that have the biggest impact on your overall development. Decisions like: Hitting the snooze button rather than getting up and working out; running personal errands in the middle of the afternoon rather than making some additional phone calls; eating a candy bar instead of an apple.

Goals organize and energize your days. They provide purpose to your activities and help you set priorities. But *setting* goals is just the first step. Most people get at least that far. Where they falter is in the commitment required to actually *attain* those goals. Goal attainment requires vigilant attention to little daily decisions. Each time you are faced with a choice, ask yourself, "Which choice will bring me closer to my goal?"

#66 Details Make the Difference

"You must see your goals clearly and specifically before you can set out for them. Hold them in your mind until they become second nature."

LES BROWN

When you want something, don't be vague about it. Write your goals with clarity, precision and vivid description. Make them come alive on the page. The more specific you are about what you want the more likely you are to get it. The difference between wishes and goals lies in the details.

Take two people who want to buy a house. The first person says "Yeah, I'd like to buy a house in the next few months." The second person says, "I'd like to buy a house in the Royal Oaks subdivision by the end of April. I'm looking for a brick split-level ranch with four bedrooms and two bathrooms with an attached garage and a big backyard for my dog." Who is more likely to get exactly what they want?

The more details you can ascribe to your goals the more excited you will be to accomplish them. If you don't have enthusiasm about your goals they are just words on paper. You must vividly imagine them to the point of almost being able to touch them. This is the fuel that will propel you forward during times of adversity. If you aren't emotionally attached to your goals, then perhaps they aren't the right goals for you in the first place.

Goal setting is a requirement for any successful business. The more vividly you can picture your goals the more power they have to pull you through the obstacles that will inevitably present themselves. Setting goals is the easy part – staying the course during the tough times requires an extra level of commitment. Being able to see the details of the accomplished goal can be the difference between success and failure.

#67 Everything Compounds

"Confidence doesn't come out of nowhere. It's the result of something...hours and days and weeks and years of constant work and dedication."

ROGER STAUBACH

Money isn't the only thing that compounds; so does everything else in life. All that you do (or don't do) today will add up to a cumulative total at some point in the future. All the little daily decisions, ones you may not even realize you are making, add to the ultimate result. If you get a little better every day, you won't have to worry about making dramatic breakthroughs in times of panic. You may have a big breakthrough every so often, but you won't have to rely on them for forward progress. Evaluate your performance daily, both professionally and personally, to see if you've grown, even a tiny bit. Keep in mind it's all about forward progress, not perfection.

There's always room for a big leap forward now and then, but small steps forward every day add up quickly. Don't worry about hitting a home run every day, just work to get on base. It's the base hits that set the stage for the home runs. A home run isn't as valuable if it hasn't been preceded by a couple of base hits.

It's not as glamorous or exciting to get a little better each day, but the final result is much more solid and powerful. Think about how the Grand Canyon was formed. That natural wonder is the result of millions of years of unnoticed erosion, not one big explosion. Of course, it won't take you quite that long to enjoy the fruits of your labor, but you get the point.

#68 Keep Your Word

"Example is not the main thing in influencing others, it is the only thing."

ALBERT SCHWEITZER

One of the most powerful ways you can build self-esteem and credibility is to always do what you say you will do. This character trait can be developed through disciplined effort. When you say something, people will make a judgment based on whether or not you follow through. If you don't take your word seriously enough to follow through, why would your prospects and clients take you seriously? Or your family and friends for that matter?

If you say you are going to call at a particular time, do it. If you say you are going to be somewhere at a certain time, be there on time. Watch the excuses you make for yourself when it comes to not keeping your word. They are probably similar to the excuses you hear from others.

When you say you will do something, you want others to think "Well, that's done" rather than "Well, he or she has said that many times before and never followed through, why would this time be any different?" Keeping your word is something you have opportunities to demonstrate many times on a daily basis. People remember both the large and small ways in which you did or didn't follow through. The long-term effect of becoming person of your word is the respect of others and more importantly, your self-respect.

#69 Whatever It Takes

"Sometimes it is not enough to do your best, sometimes you must do what is required."

T. LYNN PREWITT, CLU

This is an eloquent way of saying you must do whatever it takes to attain your goal even when you think you cannot take one more step. If it means going the extra mile or the extra 10 miles, you do it because you are committed to the point that you won't quit until the job is done.

Begin to think in terms of doing what is required – not falling short of the goal and feeling good because you did your "best." Most people have no idea what they are capable of doing until they are on fire with a commitment to a meaningful goal. Then creativity really kicks in and when you ask yourself "How can I get this done?" your brain will begin to provide answers even when you aren't thinking about it consciously.

Every time you feel that you have hit the wall, clear your mind and think about what else you could do about your goal. Sometimes if you just spend five or 10 minutes quietly thinking, something may pop into your head that surprises you. If you are not vigilant and disciplined, you will tend to spend this time creating excuses about why you did your best and still missed the goal. Seldom do people really, truly give it their all in pursuit of something. Think about what kind of place the world would be if everyone in it gave 100 percent to everything they did. Dare to lead the charge.

#70 Dream, Feel, Think, Plan, Act

"First comes thought, then organization of that thought into ideas and plans, then transformation of those plans into reality. The beginning, as you will observe, is in your imagination."

NAPOLEAN HILL

Living by design starts with a dream. The dream generates a feeling which gets you thinking. Thinking leads to a plan which then necessitates action. Dream, feel, think, plan, act – this combination of steps leads to powerful results. You are now in a business with unlimited potential for growth and achievement; don't waste the opportunity by playing small.

These steps engage both the emotional and logical parts of your brain. Enthusiasm and energy about what you want are critical but you also have to have a plan to accomplish your dream. Otherwise it's just pie in the sky. It can be an exciting topic of conversation for a while, but when those around you realize you are not doing anything about your dream, interest wanes. Sometimes all it takes is writing down the dream to begin to make it seem more achievable. Breaking your dream goal down into specific steps can make it seem more manageable.

Suppose you get the idea to qualify for the Million Dollar Round Table in your first year. For a brand new agent, this is a lofty goal. So you have the dream and start to feel excited about it. Then logic takes over and the thinking part of your brain tells you this just isn't possible. But you start to form a plan anyway and figure out how much premium you need to submit on a weekly basis, how many prospects it will take to generate the number of required factfinders to yield the necessary closes to get to the premium. And then you begin to execute the plan one step at a time.

Dream big, then feel the excitement, think about the possibilities, plan your strategy and take some small step in that direction. It won't be a perfect process, but before you know it, you'll be on your way to what seemed like an impossible goal at one time.

#71 Desire and Strategy

"Vision just passes the time. Vision with action can change the" Vision without action is merely a dream. Action without world!"*

JOEL ARTHUR BARKER

It is not enough to simply want something badly. To make things happen, you must have two elements – desire and strategy. Think about having both the Tinman's heart and the Scarecrow's brain from the "Wizard of Oz." Both desire and strategy must be present to make progress. If you have the intense desire to accomplish something but no strategy, it's just wishful thinking. You are an excited agent running around with great enthusiasm but no plan. Then nothing gets done, and you end up not being very excited any more.

Conversely, if you have a great plan but no burning desire to get it done, then you are probably taking on a goal that isn't important to you in order to please someone else. You end up a methodical producer who has little emotional connection to what you are trying to get done and therefore not much chance of getting it done. When you are on fire with the desire to accomplish a specific goal and a strategy for attaining it, then you have set the stage for tremendous accomplishment.

There are usually certain benchmarks that your company's management team will want you to accomplish as a new agent. There are also typically some minimums that you have to accomplish if you want to keep your contract. Both of these situations can cause you to find yourself working on a goal that isn't of your own choosing. In this case, you will have a plan but not the burning desire. Look at this as a temporary situation, and when you accomplish the result, then you can get back to your own particular goals. Over the course of your career, you will want to be so successful that you don't even know what the minimums are because you are so far beyond them.

#72 Streaks and Slumps

"No man ever achieved worthwhile success who did not, at one time or another, find himself with at least a foot hanging well over the brink of failure."

NAPOLEAN HILL

In baseball it is not uncommon for players to experience streaks and slumps. A player may have a hot bat and hit safely in 20 consecutive games while another may have remained hitless over the same time period. The player on a streak will ultimately strike out or be thrown out, and the player in the slump will ultimately get on base if he keeps getting up to bat. Both players may end up with successful seasons because of the large number of opportunities to change the averages by making adjustments. That's the advantage of having 162 games in a season.

This business works the same way. Through the sheer number of opportunities you create for yourself, you can change your averages over time. You won't be on a streak forever, nor will you be in a slump forever - whether it's phoning, prospecting, closing or another activity. One bad day, week or even month will not ruin your career, even though in that moment it feels like it will never end. It's the stringing together of many bad days, weeks or months that become your undoing. It is even possible to survive a bad year if you have enough time in the business. Chris, a top producer for several years, had a $100,000 premium reversal one year and still had a net result of over $500,000 of premium for the year. He wasn't happy about it but knew he could overcome it the next year.

Don't get too smug when you're on a streak and don't get too depressed when you are in a slump. Just remember baseball and realize there are many more games ahead of you in which you can impact the averages.

#73 Assume Nothing

"People don't plan to fail – they fail to plan."

WILLIAM SIEGAL

You are often the only reason people address their financial issues. Think about how often you have known what to do, but not taken action. It could be exercising, making your phone calls, prospecting, eating your vegetables or anything else that would benefit you. Then multiply that by thousands, and you now have the mindset of the marketplace. Most prospects that you would want as clients are intelligent, motivated, successful people, yet they have not addressed the basic issues of financial security. They have a vague idea that something needs to be done, but have not taken the steps to initiate any planning.

That is why you are so important. Until relentlessly confronted by the need to plan, most people will procrastinate. Agents often assume that the more successful a person is the more planning they must have already done. This has re-peatedly proven to be untrue. The most successful and intelligent people in the world still need another human being to guide them in areas in which they are not the experts. You are the catalyst that moves people to action regarding their planning.

Once agents eliminate the assumption that successful people have already done their planning and call on them, they are often surprised at what hasn't been done. This is why on-line companies will never take the place of human beings. On-line companies can't tap someone on the shoulder and say, "You'd better take a look at where you are headed financially." On-line companies cannot relentlessly confront the issues that will ultimately benefit people's lives.

A good agent can mean the difference between financial ruin and financial security for families, businesses and individuals.

#74 Clients First, Always

"We are not here merely to make a living. We are here to enrich the world with a finer spirit of hope and achievement – and we impoverish ourselves if we forget the errand."

WOODROW WILSON

When you are most fearful, having a "clients first" focus is a habit that can turn things around. A large dose of discipline is required to develop this habit. In times of greatest fear, the tendency will be to go inward and focus on yourself. Remember, thoughts are like plants – if you focus on them and feed them, they will grow. Constantly thinking about your fears and challenges will simply cause them to grow. Redirect your focus away from yourself and your fears and toward serving your clients and impacting their lives. You will find yourself thinking more positive thoughts and generating more great ideas.

Being truly client-centered is imperative to long-term success in the financial services business. This doesn't mean being a martyr or ignoring your own needs, but simply putting your clients first. Do this enough times and you will generate much more than you need. Zig Ziglar, motivational expert, says if you help enough other people get what they want, you will get what you want.

If you operate out of a genuine heart for people even when they test you the most, they will sense that, and you will be more likely to bring them on as a client. Do this enough times, and suddenly you have a base of many loyal clients. However, this does not change the concept that not everyone will buy from you – it simply ensures that even those who don't buy will have higher regard for you.

#75 Pushing Prospects Off the Fence

"Leading people is a responsibility, not a perk. To whomever much is given, much is required."
JOHN MAXWELL

By choosing this career, you have put yourself in a leadership position. You will lead people in their decision-making in critical areas. This requires that you have the fortitude to confront people when they are procrastinating and that you ask people to take action. This may seem like common sense, but many agents will present the solution and wait for the prospect to be bowled over with excitement and initiate the next step themselves.

Human nature dictates that most people will procrastinate, particularly when it means sacrificing immediate pleasure for long-term gain. This is where most agents are afraid to press forward. They allow people to sit on the fence for fear of jeopardizing the relationship. They assume that if they push too hard the prospect will scrap the entire process and any hope of a sale will be destroyed forever. Consequently, several meetings later there is still no decision, and the agent is now chasing the prospect in frustration.

Confronting people with their inaction may make them uncomfortable, but when it is done out of belief and passion, it will ultimately garner respect for the agent. Most people want someone to lead them in areas where they do not have the expertise to make informed decisions.

Relationships built on trust can withstand resistance and even conflict and will grow stronger as a result. If the entire relationship is at risk because an agent pushed too hard, then the relationship was not solid in the first place. If you are operating out of a deep belief in your process and products, you will be willing to risk the relationship to get the job done, knowing that your prospect will be better off as a result.

#76 Service with a Smile

"To give real service you must add something which cannot be bought or measured with money, and that is sincerity and integrity."

ABRAHAM LINCOLN

Building your own business requires a tremendous amount of sales activity. Magic happens when a sale is made. The excitement of the chase, overcoming objections, the thrill of accomplishment when a prospect writes a check – all these things get the blood pumping. However, many ambitious salespeople stop there. The way to truly distinguish yourself is to provide superior service after the sale. Delivering the policies you sold is the first step.

Some agents have stacks of undelivered policies in their offices. A common reason for this is a fear that clients will change their minds about their purchases or lower the amounts they originally bought, causing commission reversals to the agent. In reality, clients are far less likely to reverse their decisions if they feel they have an agent they can count on to follow through and keep in touch after the sale.

Ignoring this important aspect of the sales cycle diminishes future sales opportunities. One company's statistics indicate that a client will buy on average five to seven more times over the course of the relationship. This assumes a level of service that reflects your sincerity about helping the client. Policy delivery appointments are often dismissed as non-productive. On the contrary, these appointments provide opportunities to prospect, to open additional cases, to cement the relationship, to reinforce the reasons for the sale, to lay out mutual expectations and to prove to the client that you are unique in your sales process.

When you are tempted to skip or delay this part of the sales cycle, remember you are sending a message to your clients that once they have written a check they become less important to you. To be among the top performers, you must adopt the mentality that your prospects are as important at the end of the sales cycle as they were in the beginning.

#77 Computers Can't Convey Compassion

"No one ever attains eminent success by simply doing what is required of him; it is the amount and excellence of what is over and above the required that determines the greatest of ultimate distinction."
CHARLES KENDALL ADAMS

The Internet is not going to replace you as an agent. First of all, in this particular industry people seldom buy the products on their own initiative. Most aren't even thinking about insurance and other financial products until it's too late. That's one of the reasons this business is so difficult. You are overcoming resistance at every turn from the initial phone call to the close. It is your belief and persistence that moves prospects to action. The computer can't do that. It can do no more than provide information. Since we know that people don't buy our products without being emotionally moved, you are not in danger of becoming an extinct species.

What happens when a client needs to make a claim? Will the computer show up with a check? What happens when a client needs service? Will the Internet provide it in a timely manner? These are the things people don't think about when they are wrapped up in saving a few dollars. In the time of need, would a client really prefer to "surf the net" seeking service or know they have an agent they can count on?

In this technological era of cell phones, wireless Internet, instant messaging and endless voice mail mazes, people crave human contact more than ever. Seldom can you make a phone call to a company anymore and actually get a live human being. Technology is powerful and useful in the right situations but sometimes good, old-fashioned human contact is irreplaceable.

The business will always be about personal contact and relationships built on trust and service. Your clients know they can count on you to be there when times are tough. They don't need a hard drive – they need a heart.

#78 Tame Your Technology

"Congealed thinking is the forerunner of failure...make sure you are always receptive to new ideas."

GEORGE CRANE

In a world where writing checks and using pay phones are fast becoming obsolete activities, it is important to be technologically attuned. Investing in up-to-date technology is much like hiring the right assistant. In and of itself it won't make you successful, but it enhances your odds by making your work more mobile. Having a laptop computer and a cell phone won't replace the hard work of phoning and seeing people; it will simply enable you to work more efficiently and effectively, creating more time to phone and see more people.

Technology presents yet another opportunity for you to take financial risk and invest in your business. There are an overwhelming number of options when it comes to technology so it pays to do a little homework. Find out what your company offers by way of computers, long distance service, personal digital assistants, etc. Sometimes companies provide financing or discounts on the brands their software supports. Be careful if you are going outside the recommended company options, as other brands may not support the software your company requires for presentation materials.

If you are hesitant about technology (i.e., remember when having an electric typewriter in college meant you were technologically advanced?), you need to at least learn the basics, particularly if you are working with young people today who had computers in kindergarten and cell phones in middle school.

There will always be cutting-edge technology that makes whatever you just bought obsolete in mere months. Don't spend your energy or resources trying to keep up with the latest and greatest; you'll wear yourself out. Even if you are a year or two or three behind the newest version you are still in the game.

#79 Meetings: To Go or Not To Go

"Everyone needs constant education and training. The more you keep yourself informed, the better your instincts and decision-making capabilities."

LINDA CONWAY

Attending meetings seems destined to provoke complaints among busy sales professionals. "There's not enough time in the day," or "I could be out seeing people," or "Not another one" are just a few of the battle cries heard when a meeting pops up on the calendar. Your attitude toward meetings will have a huge impact on the value you get from them.

You cannot act on an idea you didn't hear because you skipped a meeting. Getting information secondhand just doesn't have the same impact. Investing the time to attend all meetings designed for your benefit will yield great rewards. A single idea can change the way you think and consequently change your business. Meetings are a great way to learn from the experts.

Look at every meeting from two perspectives: What value can I get from this meeting and what value can I contribute to this meeting. People too often go to meetings thinking only of the first part of that equation. Even something as simple as asking a question can add value to a meeting. If you have a question, chances are so does someone else in the audience.

You cannot operate your business in a vacuum – you need a steady diet of inspiration and ideas from outside yourself. Great agents attend their mentor meetings, agency meetings, company meetings and industry meetings. They do it because they know that they can't possibly get all the information they need on their own and because being around others who are enthusiastic and willing to learn can be the biggest benefit of all.

#80 Pass the Follow-up Test

"The personal touch is so rare a commodity today, it becomes a standout."

HARVEY MACKAY

Follow up. It's the one thing you can do to immediately distinguish yourself in the eyes of your prospects and clients. This is so deceptively simple that many agents dismiss it with a shrug. Don't underestimate the power of following up. It does two things. First, it tells your prospects and clients that you are dependable and will call when you say you will call. Second, it cements in your own mind that you are a person of integrity and persistence.

The amazing thing about follow up is how few people actually do it. Whether this is born of fear or carelessness, it is common to hear from salespeople once, to ask them to call back later and then to never hear from them again. Agents in particular are fearful of seeming pushy or desperate. In fact, as long as people are giving you permission to call them back, you are simply following orders. Consider it a test – maybe the prospect is wondering if you, like so many others, will simply disappear into the woodwork upon hearing your first "no."

Those who don't meet with you initially but give permission to keep in touch will be surprised, perhaps even stunned, to actually hear from you three or six months later. If they don't want to hear from you again, make them say so.

Successful prospects typically have someone who fields their calls in the office. The smart way around this dilemma is to work through this gatekeeper. Every time you are asked to call back, actually doing so will impress the gatekeeper and may be the best way to get the word to your prospect that you follow through. If the gatekeeper has the ability to make appointments and he or she sees that you are reliable, you have a much better chance of getting in to see your prospect. Never underestimate the power of following up; it is often the reason for getting an appointment or a sale, even if it happens down the road.

#81 Do the Right Thing

"The truth of the matter is that you always know the right thing to do. The hard part is doing it."
GENERAL NORMAN SCHWARZKOPF

It doesn't seem necessary to have to write about doing the right thing, does it? But think for a minute about the presidents, CEOs, sports heroes and others who, in the moments when they thought no one was looking, didn't do the right thing. Think about the consequences of their actions. A series of bad decisions they hoped no one would ever discover led to their downfall or a permanently tarnished image.

There will be many opportunities for you to take shortcuts. Here's a common scenario: You missed a signature on an application and thought it would be OK to sign for your client rather than take the time to go back and get it. After all, they agreed to buy from you so they must trust you, right? This particular deed is a career-ending move and can cause you to lose your license. But no one will ever know, you say. You will know. Misdeeds and mindsets like this one will erode your confidence and ultimately end your career on a sour note. Doing the wrong thing even once makes it easier to do it again, especially if you don't get caught.

You have countless opportunities every day to do the right thing. You know what the right thing is because it often makes you groan and say "Do I have to?" as in the case of a missed signature. Don't waste time creating justifications about why you did the wrong thing – do the right thing at every opportunity and the results will compound into abundant integrity and respect over your career and your life.

#82 Operator Error

"Don't be afraid to fail. Don't waste energy trying to cover up failure. Learn from your failures and go on to the next challenge. It's okay. If you're not failing, you're not growing."

H. STANLEY JUDD

When you have challenges in this business, you would be wise to look inward first, then examine your external circumstances. Challenged by lack of premium? Examine your commitment as measured by how much of your product you own. Challenged by quality of prospects? Examine the way you are living your life – you will attract people fairly close to your own circumstances. Many of the answers to your success are within you, not within a textbook, additional license or new designation.

It is important that you become technically proficient in your chosen career; however, all the technical knowledge in the world will not replace the internal examination of your beliefs, values and commitments. Most changes in your business begin with internal reflection. You will be fighting an uphill battle if you neglect to self-examine before chasing technical answers.

When you have an internal breakthrough, then the technical answers will surface and make more sense. It takes courage to look inward which is why many people actively avoid it. If you don't like what you find, chances are good others have already noticed and it may be hindering your business opportunities.

Develop the habit of looking inward first and you will have many more breakthroughs than someone who continues to amass technical expertise yet can't understand why people don't respond positively and become clients.

#83 Watch Your Self-Talk

"The happiness of your life depends upon the quality of your thoughts, therefore guard accordingly and take care that you entertain no thoughts unsuitable to virtue and reasonable nature."

MARCUS AURELIUS

Your brain is wired to answer the questions it encounters, including the ones you ask yourself. So it becomes important to watch what questions you ask yourself. For example, if you ask yourself "How could I have been so stupid?" your brain will begin to answer that question with a list of reasons about why you were indeed so stupid.

On the other hand, when you ask yourself something like "How can I make this happen?" your brain is trained to answer that one, too. You will be surprised when your brain kicks into gear and begins to come up with ideas you didn't even know you had. People tend to spend far more time indulging in negative thoughts and questions than positive ones. If you can catch yourself even a fraction of the time, you will begin to change that trend and suddenly have more ideas and solutions than you ever thought possible.

Sometimes your brain can try too hard to come up with answers. For example, you're asked a question and you know the answer, but just can't come up with it right at that moment. The harder you try, the more elusive it gets. But if you stop thinking about it for a while, when you least expect it, the answer pops out. This is the miracle of your brain. Make sure you are feeding it questions that require positive answers so when ideas are popping out they are useful and not detrimental to your forward progress.

#84 Growing Pains

"Knowing others is intelligence; knowing yourself is true wisdom."

LAO TZU

You will get to know yourself like never before as a result of choosing this business. It rapidly brings to the surface all the issues you've managed to avoid about yourself so far. The specific issues are different for each individual, but the phenomenon holds true across the board. If your financial situation is a mess, you will find it hard to make sales until you clean it up. If you don't trust others, you will find it difficult to get others to trust you and buy from you. If you don't take personal responsibility for your circumstances, you will find it easy to buy excuses from others.

The nature of the work requires that you be keenly self-aware as you go into the marketplace and help others to address their issues. Personal growth is not optional. You will come face to face with yourself on a regular basis. Most of the answers you will seek externally will be found internally. This kind of growth can be painful and awkward, and often you will not like what you find. Those who have the courage to address these issues will ultimately build strong, successful businesses. Those who don't won't last long. The marketplace is objective and uncaring. It will respond to those who grow and will deny those who don't.

Make a habit of checking in with yourself first as problems arise. See what issues you need to address within yourself. Then you will be much more able to deal with the external issues. Think of it as free therapy. You will learn more about yourself in this business than in almost any other. It is sometimes painful, sometimes humorous, sometimes sobering, but always enlightening.

#85 Live Your Mission

"There is no paycheck that can equal the feeling of contentment that comes from being the person you were meant to be."

OPRAH WINFREY

In a perfect world, who you are (your values, where you find your energy) and what you do (your tasks) would be in sync. They would be so closely linked that no one could tell the difference. You would wake up every day with the feeling that you are doing what you were born to do. You want to choose a career that is harmonious with what you believe, what you enjoy and what you want to accomplish in the world.

Many people go through life getting up in the morning and feeling like they just have to get through the day so they can go home and be themselves again. It's extremely stressful to have to fake your way through day after day. When you truly love what you do because it expresses who you are, then you are on your way to a fulfilling life. You are living your mission.

You can easily recognize those around you who are living their mission – they light up from the inside and have an energy and enthusiasm about their work. They stumble and fail as much, if not more, than anyone yet they never lose sight of themselves or their vision. There are veteran agents who have been in the business for 40 or more years who are now working with the grown grandchildren of their original clients. How's that for living a mission?

Of course, you won't love all the aspects of what you do – there's always what's referred to as the "dirty 30" which is the 30 percent of your job that has to be done but doesn't really light you up. You tolerate it because the other 70 percent is your mission.

Very few people start out in this career believing it is what they were born to do. Those who stay with it and see the good they can do in people's lives are the ones who ultimately say "I couldn't imagine doing anything else."

#86 Get a Life – Part 1

"Enjoy yourself. It's later than you think."

CHINESE PROVERB

It's important to enjoy your work, and it's also important to enjoy the rest of your life. Becoming one dimensional as you build a career is just that – flat. Building in time to relax and pursue outside interests will actually make your work more meaningful and enjoyable. If you are single with no kids, this would be an excellent time to cultivate or further a favorite hobby. This gives you a much broader variety of topics to discuss when meeting with prospects and clients.

If you have a family, spend time with them. You never regain time lost with your children. When you have children, you are teaching them something with every choice you make. They learn more from observing what you do than from hearing what you say.

Outside interests enhance your work, not detract from it. If you aren't taking care of yourself, it's difficult to effectively help others. Spending every waking moment panic-stricken about working more will just keep you in a small, fearful world. Get involved in your community; include a variety of people in your social circle. Stay connected to friends who are not in the business.

Stay focused and work smart to keep your business from sinking during the hours you spend with family, friends, hobbies or other interests. Don't wait until the end of your life to enjoy it.

#87 Get a Life – Part 2

"You can discover more about a person in an hour of play than in a year of conversation."

PLATO

One of the essential ingredients in mental toughness is recovery time. Think about any sporting event – baseball, basketball, football, hockey, soccer – they all allow recovery time during intense performances. Whether it's a substitution, a time out or a change of inning, the players are allowed to catch their breath so they can begin again with a fresh cycle of peak energy.

It's a physical fact that you cannot operate at peak performance levels if you are exhausted. It is better to take the time to rest and recover than to continue to push yourself to the brink of ill health. It would be ironic and sad to spend your life in hot pursuit of your goals and then be too ill and exhausted to enjoy the rewards.

Understand, however, this assumes you are working at peak capacity when you are working. This doesn't apply if you are working four or five hours at 50 percent and then taking the rest of the day off. You must be attuned to when you are really exhausted versus simply feeling unmotivated.

Bottom line: Work hard, play hard, and rest often.

#88 Walk a Mile in Your Shoes

"A strong body makes the mind strong."

THOMAS JEFFERSON

The first thing that gets abandoned when you come into this business is usually a commitment to your health and physical fitness. You are so panicked about succeeding that you feel you cannot afford to take the time to exercise and think about what you are eating. Every waking moment must be concentrated on your business.

The irony of this thinking is: If you aren't taking care of yourself, you will be ill-equipped to help others. Think about the airplane flight attendant on the last trip you took. Part of their litany on every single flight is the instruction that you must put on your *own* oxygen mask first before attempting to help others secure theirs. That metaphor applies to life in many aspects. You will be no help to others if you aren't getting enough oxygen, literally or otherwise.

This contradicts the popular notion that helping others requires continual self-sacrifice. While that may apply some-times, it is not a constant truth. The more energy and vitality you have personally, the more you can give to those around you.

When you are in top physical form, you are much more likely to be in peak performance mode when you are working. If you are constantly tired, stressed and gaining weight you will feel negative much of the time and small setbacks will affect you much more intensely.

Taking the time to exercise will be one of the best invest-ments of your time you ever make. Think about it: Your busi-ness isn't going to fall apart if you spend 30 minutes a day in the gym or running through your neighborhood. On the contrary, the return on your investment will be more energy, clearer thinking and a better, more powerful image of yourself. This will only help your prospects and clients.

#89 What Goes Around Comes Around

"Quiet minds cannot be perplexed or frightened, but go on in fortune or misfortune at their own private pace like a clock during a thunderstorm."

ROBERT LOUIS STEVENSON

Most things in life are cyclical. This business is no exception. Football coach Lou Holtz once said, "I've been on the top, I've been on the bottom, and I'll be both places again." The key to navigating the inevitable roller coaster ride is to maintain consistent activity.

For example, if you ask five people to buy your product each week, there will be weeks where everyone will say "no." However, if week after week you continue to ask five people to buy your product, things will come full circle and some will say "yes," maybe even all five. You are controlling the one constant factor which is your behavior. You continue to ask five people to buy every week regardless of their response. This can also apply to asking for prospects, making phone calls or scheduling appointments.

You cannot control how people respond; you cannot predict who will say "yes" and who will say "no" so you must continue to ask everyone. Then, amid the emotional chaos of their varying responses, you will remain the steady force who presses forward, confident in the knowledge that the cycle will complete time after time, and the results will ultimately even out in your favor.

#90 Take a Deep Breath

"Emotional competence is the single most important personal quality that each of us must develop and access to experience a breakthrough."

DOUG LENNICK

A creative church sign reads "Strive to have the wisdom of Solomon and the patience of Job." Sage advice in any endeavor, but particularly in a business like this one, where dealing with human behavior and emotions can try even the most patient of souls.

In the early days of your career, you will experience emotional ups and downs like never before. The key to managing this is to recognize your emotional reactions and insert a pause before moving to action. Feel, think about what you feel, and then take action. The simple step of stopping and thinking about what you feel before you respond can mean the difference between saying or doing something you may regret later and adopting a more mature response.

Children respond immediately to what they are feeling. They cry, scream, rage or throw tantrums the minute the feeling occurs. As they grow older, they learn to control their reactions. This is the essence of maturity. It doesn't mean you don't continue to have feelings or ignore them. It simply means you have the self-control to recognize that you need to think clearly before responding or reacting.

You will earn the respect of clients, prospects, peers and everyone else with your ability to remain calm and rational in the face of emotional situations. It doesn't mean you behave like a robot or don't ever show your emotions; but rather that you are capable of calming a situation instead of escalating it. Your ability to exhibit maturity and leadership will go a long way in establishing you as the preferred advisor to your clients.

#91 Stress Is a State of Mind

"If you're happy in what you're doing, you'll like yourself, you'll have inner peace. And if you have that, along with physical health, you will have had more success than you could have possibly imagined."
                                                           JOHNNY CARSON

Stress is not a tangible thing – it is the result of your thinking process. Most stress occurs when you make daily decisions that are not aligned with your priorities. For example if spending time at home with your family is a high priority for you, but you spend all your evenings and weekends working, you will have a high level of stress. You may feel that in a career like this you have no choice but to work every waking moment. The truth is that if you take time to be with your family three weeknights out of five then you will be refreshed, energized and more effective on the two evenings you do work.

If you know from day to day what is truly important to you (and this differs from person to person) and you make your decisions accordingly, then you will have very little bad stress in your life. Some stress is good for you because it creates adrenaline and pushes you forward. Positive stress propels you to double-check details and practice presentations to do well. But when you can't sleep or don't eat or constantly feel sick, then negative stress is getting the better of you.

Learn to distinguish between positive stress and negative stress. Let the positive stress propel you forward and let the negative stress serve as a warning sign that something is out of balance in your priorities.

#92 The More, The Merrier

"A company's character is known by the people it keeps."
JOHN RUSKIN

Take a minute to think about how you came to be in this business. Perhaps your own agent referred you, perhaps you were referred by an agent other than your own, maybe you attended a campus career fair or you put your resume on one of the Internet services and received a call.

According to a 2003 USA Today poll, 61 percent of those asked said they obtained their current position through word of mouth or networking. In other words, someone referred them. Typically, the same dynamic applies to the financial services industry. The most successful agents were initially referred into the business by other successful agents.

You may be thinking, "Hey, it's not my job to find other agents – that's the recruiter's job." Technically, you're right but think about it this way: Wouldn't you love to have a hand in choosing the colleagues with whom you will be working every day? Wouldn't it be great to see someone's life change because you made them aware of a great opportunity? If you truly believe this business offers a tremendous opportunity for personal and financial success, why wouldn't you want others to experience it?

The same objections that your prospects and clients have when you ask for referred leads often come out of your own mouth when a recruiter asks you for referred leads. Don't let fear of competition or a scarcity mentality stop you from referring someone to your recruiter. You could be changing someone's destiny just as yours was changed when you took on the challenge of this career.

#93 Be Courageous, Not Casual

*"Courageous risks are life giving, they help you grow,
make you brave and better than you think you are."*
JOAN L. CURCIO

You cannot choose to be in this business and be casual.
It's been said, "Casualness leads to casualties." Focus, commitment and high energy are requirements for success in any
endeavor, particularly this one. Trade casual for courageous.

Would you want to do business with anyone who
projected a casual attitude about themselves, their lives, their
work or their commitments in general? If your doctor had a
casual attitude about your health, would you continue to see
him or her? If your accountant had a casual attitude about
your finances, wouldn't you fire him or her?

You are faced with a thousand tiny decisions every day:
Do you approach them casually, unaware that you are even
making them? Or are you thoughtful about every decision you
make and act with courage and conviction on even the smallest
of issues? To rise above the crowd of average people you must
train yourself to pay attention to the daily decisions you make.
Every decision is like a pebble thrown in a pond – the ripples
carry the impact of your decision far and wide.

This fits into the broader concept of living by design or
by default. The decision to go to a hockey game on a Sunday
night and have a few beers will impact your energy Monday
morning, potentially impacting the rest of your week.

Pay close attention to your daily decisions. This will help
you see when and where you get off track. The compounded
effect of more conscious and courageous small, daily decisions
will be the more powerful, deliberate life you create for yourself
and others.

#94 Ring Out the Old, Ring In the New

"You can clutch the past so tightly to your chest that it leaves your arms too full to embrace the present."

JAN GLIDEWELL

Here's the number one reality of being in this business: It forces you to grow both personally and professionally. One of the realities of growth is that it often necessitates leaving behind some of the people, places and things that created great comfort for you. As you grow, you will embrace new ideas, new habits and new relationships. If those around you choose not to grow, the gap will widen as time goes by.

It's painful and often scary to let go of old friends and old ways of thinking and being. But pain usually precipitates growth, and once you're on the other side you realize that the rewards are worth it. You have to keep reminding yourself that everyone has the capacity to grow and develop themselves; some people simply choose not to do it.

It's a risk to let go of old patterns, attitudes and relationships because they are comfortable and most importantly, predictable. Everything in life prepares you for the next thing. As you are letting go, you are making room for new ideas, opportunities and people. As much as you would love to embrace new things while holding on to the tried and true, it simply doesn't work that way. You have to let go to truly grow, knowing that the risk is worth the reward.

#95 Keep It on the Books

"The quality of a man's life is in direct proportion to his commitment to excellence, regardless of his chosen field of endeavor."

VINCE LOMBARDI

An important measure of your long-term success is how long your clients' policies stay in force. In the industry, this is called your persistency (or from the negative side, your lapse rate.) For example, if your persistency is 98 percent, then your lapse rate is 2 percent. This means that 98 percent of your policies stayed in force over the time period measured. Obviously the goal is 100 percent persistency or a 0 percent lapse rate.

The best way to keep business from lapsing is to write and service solid business in the first place. This begins with a quality prospect who, according to industry expert Al Granum, is intelligent, responsible and has good economic potential. Then in the factfinding process you establish rapport, begin to build trust and find out what the client wants and needs.

A thorough analysis of clients' needs and consistent service after the sale will keep your clients loyal to you over your career. Selling a product based on clients' documented needs, not because you have to pay your bills, will help you build your business. Your clients know that you have their best interests in mind. Every opportunity for service is a chance to gently remind your clients why they bought from you in the first place. Frequency of contact keeps your name in front of your clients and makes them less likely to buy from anyone else.

You will see agents who spend a great deal of their time trying to track down clients who haven't paid their monthly premium or who won't return phone calls. Chances are good that the agent didn't do a good job factfinding, building trust or forming a relationship. The client may have bought the product but didn't necessarily buy the reasons they needed it. Now they have buyer's remorse. You can prevent this by keeping your clients' needs foremost in your mind and keeping in touch regularly.

#96 You Can't Do It By Yourself – Part 1

"It's amazing what you can accomplish if you do not care who gets the credit."

HARRY S TRUMAN

There will come a time after you've begun to experience some success that you will need to hire an assistant. Usually within the first six months to a year, you will have a tremendous amount of paperwork and service work to do. Rather than lean on this as an excuse to avoid the hard work of high activity or to fill your days with administrative tasks, begin looking for someone to help you.

Just as you prefer to build your business with referred leads, you might have better results finding a quality candidate if you ask your friends and clients to keep their eyes and ears open rather than rely solely on blind ads. The temptation will be to hire someone as inexpensively as possible. Remember, you get what you pay for. If you hire your next-door neighbor's high school daughter or your best friend's unemployed cousin for $6 an hour, chances are you won't get much more than clerical assistance. It is also unlikely to be a long-term relationship and you will end up searching again in the near future. It might seem like the perfect solution for everyone, but convenience doesn't always equal quality.

Some agents get lucky and find the perfect assistant on the first try; others will go through several people before finding the right fit. It's important that your assistant understand the nature of the business and be interested in helping you build your business, as well as running the day-to-day operations. It's a big step to have someone financially dependent on you. Think through your options, but don't wait until you have perfect circumstances – take the risk.

#97 You Can't Do It By Yourself – Part 2

"The reputation of a thousand years may be determined by the conduct of one hour."

JAPANESE PROVERB

You want to hire someone with the idea that it will make a tangible difference in the growth of your business, not just that you will have someone to complete applications or perform all the daily mundane tasks you don't want to do. A little planning will save you some stress later on. Figure out what you are willing to pay and list the expectations you have for this position. Then put away about three months of income for the person you hire. That way you know you will be able to pay him or her as you continue to weather the ups and downs of the business.

Pay close attention to this next sentence: Not paying your newly hired assistant because you didn't get paid or had a negative paycheck is not an option. You are now an employer who has someone financially dependent on you. This is when your planning pays off. If you have some money set aside specifically for this purpose or you have obtained a line of credit, you will be fine. If not, then you had better figure something out quickly or risk losing this person.

You may have a combination of base salary and bonuses, and the bonuses may fluctuate with the flow of business. But every pay period you must have the money to pay your assistant the salary portion you both agreed upon. Bouncing a paycheck you have written to your assistant, promising to pay them "next time" or any other deviation from a regular paycheck is unacceptable and speaks poorly to your character. If you think this is a harsh judgment, you would be correct. This is a commitment, not a convenience.

#98 Funnels and Cycles

"If you have a talent, use it in every which way possible. Don't hoard it, spend it lavishly like a millionaire intent on going broke."

BRENDAN FRANCIS

The business of financial services can be explained pretty simply using two concepts – funnels and cycles: Funnels because it will always be a business of large numbers to small numbers and cycles because it will always be a business of ups and downs that even out in the end with high activity. If you can remember these two images when you are at one of the inevitable low points, it will aid in reversing that downward spiral more quickly.

You will always have to fill the large end of the business funnel with many names to get to the few clients that will emerge from the narrow opening at the bottom. The only way to widen this narrow opening is to widen the large opening at the top. To repeat an earlier lesson: The best way to get more clients is to get more prospects, many, many more prospects – not to chase the few high-dollar prospects who in the end may or may not buy from you.

As you will recall, the business is also cyclical and the averages will work for you if you stick around long enough and keep filling the funnel. You will be up and you will be down, but you won't be either place forever. The way to smooth the road is to ride out the cycles while adding to the funnel so the lows won't be as low and the highs will be even higher.

If it helps, get a kitchen funnel and keep it on your desk next to a picture of a Ferris wheel. It will remind you of these truths and keep you moving forward.

#99 Never, Never, Never Quit

"One bout doesn't make a champion. One win or one loss isn't reflective of an entire career...champions aren't made or lost with one battle."

KELLY WILLIAMS

Persevering in the face of obstacles is a success habit. If you don't stick it out when you least feel like it, you develop the habit of quitting when things get tough. All that stuff about character being forged in times of adversity – it's true. The toughest times are the times when you learn the most about yourself and are usually followed by a breakthrough that takes you to a new level.

You'll never find the opportunities if you quit. That is not to say that staying in the business and continuing to do the same things over and over again will lead to success. Don't mistake hanging around with persevering. Persevering means sticking it out while continuing to grow and adjust to meet the challenges. It means being open to feedback, constantly self-evaluating and seeking internal as well as external solutions.

The world is full of famous examples of those who didn't quit. Think about Abraham Lincoln who lost a dozen elections before becoming one of the greatest presidents in history, Lance Armstrong who battled cancer before winning five Tour de France races, and Dan Jansen who failed in three winter Olympics before winning a gold medal and setting a world record. Reading their biographies and others' can inspire you to stay in the game.

There are also likely to be examples right in your office of ordinary people who persisted day in and day out before attaining a measure of success. Find them when you are tempted to quit because the obstacles seem overwhelming. They will shore you up and encourage you to continue.

Many times you will be tempted to give up and find some-thing easier to do. Don't live through those times alone – find someone to talk to or read something that will take your thoughts in a different direction. You are no different from the hundreds who went before you and were tempted to quit. The difference lies in whether you give in to temptation or choose to persevere.

#100 Why Do So Many Leave So Fast?

"Whenever I get to a low point, I go back to the basics. I ask myself, "Why am I doing this?" It comes down to passion."

LYN ST. JAMES

One of the most common questions people contemplating a career in financial services ask is "Why do so many people leave?" Those who quit will cite numerous reasons. "The training wasn't good enough." "I ran out of people to call." "I ran out of money." "I didn't get any support."

In reality, most people don't want to do the work required to succeed. You are building something from scratch, which requires tremendous dedication, passion and persistence. These are not natural characteristics – they must be forged through adversity and failure as well as success. Most people don't develop the patience to stick it out through the tough times.

This business requires a constant effort at self-development. You have to work harder on yourself than on your career. The majority of the population does the opposite. They work hard on their career and neglect their personal growth.

In short, the main reasons people leave the business are 1) they choose not to do the hard work; 2) they don't bounce back quickly enough from adversity; 3) they aren't receptive to coaching; 4) they don't want to develop themselves to meet the challenge; 5) intangible products are the most difficult to sell; and 6) sometimes it's just not the right fit.

Most of the reasons for failure can be overcome. Coming into this business requires a high degree of self-awareness and willingness to take personal responsibility for your circumstances. If you choose not to do what is required, do it consciously and without blaming external events for your decision.

#101 Congratulations! Now Get to Work

"Hold yourself responsible for a higher standard than anybody else expects of you. Never excuse yourself."
HENRY WARD BEECHER

If you have made it this far without being scared away, congratulations! You have chosen a noble profession that will allow you to make a difference in the world while building a wonderful life for yourself. To succeed requires constant growth on your part and as you grow, you will continually attract the kinds of prospects and clients you deserve.

You have chosen a profession that most would shy away from because of the rejection and overwhelming odds against success. But you are unique, and something inside you is up for the challenge. Always remember your personal reasons for choosing this business – these constant reminders along with your goals will overcome most obstacles.

The recruiting and selection process is much like an agent's business. Many people are interviewed but only a few are carefully selected. It's that rare fit between an individual seeking growth, challenge and opportunity and a profession that demands more of you than you ever thought possible. When the fit is right, the result is fantastic.

Carry this book with you, keep it handy in your briefcase so if someone doesn't show for an appointment, a policy gets declined or someone hangs up on you, you can refer to it and remember that these occurrences are common to all who accept the challenge. Then get back to work.

"Finish each day and be done with it. You have done what you could. Some blunders and absurdities no doubt crept in; forget them as soon as you can. Tomorrow is a new day; begin it well and serenely and with too high a spirit to be cumbered with your old nonsense."

RALPH WALDO EMERSON

Recommended Reading List

The Millionaire Mind by Thomas J. Stanley

The Millionaire Next Door by Thomas J. Stanley

Millionaire Women Next Door by Thomas J. Stanley, Ph.D.

The Excellent Investment Advisor by Nick Murray

Becoming a Person of Influence by John C. Maxwell

The 21 Indispensable Qualities of a Leader by John C. Maxwell

Thinking for a Change by John C. Maxwell

Think and Grow Rich by Napoleon Hill

Don't Sweat the Small Stuff by Richard Carlson, PhD.

Don't Sweat the Small Stuff About Money by Richard Carlson, PhD.

Storyselling for Financial Advisors by Mitch Anthony & Scott West

Reading People by Jo-Ellan Dimitrius, PhD., & Mark Mazarella

Who Moved My Cheese by Spencer Johnson, PhD.

Fifth Wave Leadership by Morris R. Shechtman

High Trust Selling by Todd Duncan

New Sales Speak by Terri Sjodin

Inner Peace for Busy People by Joan Z. Borysenko, PhD.

It's Not About the Bike by Lance Armstrong

Discover Your Sales Strengths by Benson Smith & Tony Rutigliano

How Full Is Your Bucket? by Tom Rath & Donald O. Clifton, Ph.D.

Index (by Essay Number)

About the Author

As a Development Specialist for the financial services industry, Sabine Robinson, CLU, has coached over 150 new agents for some of the most productive agencies in the Northwestern Mutual system. She began her Northwestern Mutual career in 1988 as marketing assistant and office manager for Peter W. Graff, CLU, district agent in Columbia, Mo.

In April 1990, she joined the Qualy Agency in St. Louis as assistant to John Qualy, CLU, who was then a new general agent. In September 1991, she was named Director of New Agent Development. Over the next 10 years, she set a company record for coaching the most agents with 40 paid policies in their first six months.

Sabine started her own development consulting business in July 2000 and expanded her work with agency leadership teams, new agent coaches and individual agents nationwide.

With a Bachelor of Journalism degree from the University of Missouri-Columbia, Sabine worked for the Columbia Daily Tribune for eight years prior to joining Northwestern Mutual. She is a 10-year member of Toastmasters International, a public speaking club. She also serves on the board and as a volunteer reader for Talking Tapes/Textbooks on Tape, an organization that records textbooks for the blind and learning disabled. Sabine completed her first marathon (the Marine Corps Marathon) in October 2000 and earned her Chartered Life Underwriter designation in June 2003. Sabine is a recent breast cancer survivor and currently lives in St. Louis, Mo.

To order additional copies of
Quick! The Cement Is Drying,
go to www.101bitsofwisdom.com or
contact the author at smrstlouis@msn.com.

CPSIA information can be obtained at www.ICGtesting.com
Printed in the USA
BVOW041026151112

305593BV00001B/22/A